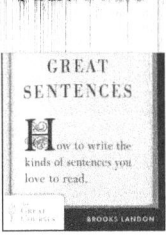

Beth Kephart
HANDLING THE TRUTH
On the Writing of Memoir
The critically acclaimed National Book Award finalist shares inspiration and practical advice for writing a memoir while discussing the form itself: how a memoir gets made, what it means to make it, and the rights of memoirists.
Gotham • 224 pp. • 978-1-592-40815-3 • $16.00

Laurie Lamson
NOW WRITE! SCIENCE FICTION, FANTASY AND HORROR
Speculative Genre Exercises from Today's Best Writers and Teachers
With writing exercises from Harlan Ellison, Piers Anthony, Ramsey Campbell, Jack Ketchum, the screenwriters of *The Twilight Zone* and *Star Trek*, and more, this volume offers a full toolbox of advice and exercises for crafting an engaging alternate reality.
Tarcher • 384 pp. • 978-0-399-16555-9 • $15.95

Sherry Ellis & Laurie Lamson, editors
NOW WRITE! MYSTERIES
Suspense, Crime, Thriller, and Other Mystery Fiction Exercises from Today's Best Writers and Teachers
The essential handbook for writers of whodunits, techno-thrillers, cozies, and everything in between, featuring never-before-published personal writing exercises from some of today's bestselling and award-winning mystery writers.
Tarcher • 384 pp. • 978-1-58542-903-5 • $14.95

Brooks Landon
BUILDING GREAT SENTENCES
How to Write the Kinds of Sentences You Love to Read
The award-winning professor draws on examples from masters of long, elegant sentences—including Virginia Woolf, Joan Didion, and Samuel Johnson—to reveal the mechanics and pleasures of language.
Plume • 288 pp. • 978-0-452-29860-6 • $16.00

Ben Yagoda
HOW TO NOT WRITE BAD
The Most Common Writing Problems and the Best Ways to Avoid Them
A comprehensive guide that lays out simple steps we can take—from proper spelling, diction, punctuation, and grammar to clarity, precision, and grace of expression—to make our writing more effective.
Riverhead • 192 pp. • 978-1-59448-848-1 • $15.00

David Corbett
THE ART OF CHARACTER
Creating Memorable Characters for Fiction, Film, and TV
In this indispensable toolkit for creating characters that come vividly to life on the page, Corbett provides an entertaining blueprint to elements of characterization, from initial inspiration to realization.
Penguin • 416 pp. • 978-0-14-312157-2 • $17.00

Meredith Maran, editor
WHY WE WRITE
20 Acclaimed Authors on How and Why They Do What They Do
Twenty of America's bestselling authors—including Isabel Allende, Sue Grafton, Sebastian Junger, Walter Mosley, and Jane Smiley—candidly share tricks, tips, and secrets of a successful writing life.
Plume • 256 pp. • 978-0-452-29815-6 • $16.00

Linda Venis, editor
INSIDE THE ROOM
Writing Television with the Pros at UCLA Extension Writers' Program
This how-to book reveals how TV shows are created and sold and takes aspiring television writers through writing a first spec script for an on-air series, creating one-hour drama and sitcom pilots, and revising scripts to meet professional standards.
Gotham • 272 pp. • 978-1-592-40811-5 • $16.00

PENGUIN GROUP (USA) Academic Marketing Department | www.penguin.com/academic

Reviewers

All essay submissions are reviewed blind by two external readers; those listed below are members of the active reader pool. We thank them for their critical contributions to scholarship in the field.

Tom Amorose
Valerie Balester
Cheryl Ball
Nicholas Behm
Patricia Belanoff
Patricia Bizzell
Bill Bolin
Darsie Bowden
Colin Brooke
Robert Brooke
Nancy Buffington
Beth Burmester
Paul Butler
Mary Ann Cain
Carol Lea Clark
Kirsti Cole
Lisa Coleman
James Comas
Juanita Rodgers Comfort
Thomas Deans
Jane Detweiler
Ronda Leathers Dively
Sidney Dobrin
Whitney Douglas
Donna Dunbar-Odom
Lynell Edwards
David Elder
Janet Carey Eldred
Michelle Eodice
Heidi Estrem
Sheryl Fontaine
Helen Fox
Tom Fox
Christy Friend
Richard Fulkerson
Catherine Gabor
Lynée Lewis Gaillet
Alice Gilliam
Maureen Daly Goggin
Angela González
Lorie Goodman
Heather Brodie Graves
Roger Graves
Paul Hanstedt
Dana Harrington
Jeanette Harris
Cynthia Haynes
Paul Heilker
Carl Herndl
Brooke Hessler
Charlotte Hogg
Bruce Horner
Sue Hum
Brian Huot
Asao Inoue
Rebecca Jackson
T. R. Johnson
Judith Kearns
Martha Kruse
bonnie kyburz
Mary Lamb
Donna LeCourt
Neal Lerner
Carrie Leverenz
Min-Zhan Lu
Brad Lucas
William Macauley
Tim Mayers
Lisa McClure
Moriah McCracken
Dan Meltzer
Ruth Mirtz
Clyde Moneyhun
Roxanne Mountford
Gerald P. Mulderig
Joan A. Mullin
Joddy Murray
Marshall Myers
Gerald Nelms
Jon Olson
Peggy O'Neill
Derek Owens
Irv Peckham
Donna Qualley
Ellen Quandahl
Kelly Ritter
Duane Roen
Randall Roorda
Blake Scott
Ellen Schendel
Carol Severino
Wendy Sharer
Steve Sherwood
Donna Strickland
William Thelin
Peter Vandenberg
Deirdre Vinyard
Zachary Waggoner
Kathleen Welch
Thomas West
Katherine Wills
Rosemary Winslow
Vershawn Ashanti Young
Janet Zepernick

composition STUDIES

Volume 41, Number 2
Fall 2013

Editor
Laura R. Micciche

Book Review Editor
Asao B. Inoue

Editorial Assistants
Christina LaVecchia
Janine Morris

Former Editors
Gary Tate
Robert Mayberry
Christina Murphy
Peter Vandenberg
Ann George
Carrie Leverenz
Brad E. Lucas
Jennifer Clary-Lemon

Advisory Board

Linda Adler-Kassner
*University of California,
Santa Barbara*

Tom Amorose
Seattle Pacific University

Chris Anson
North Carolina State University

Valerie Balester
Texas A&M University

Robert Brooke
University of Nebraska, Lincoln

Sidney Dobrin
University of Florida

Lisa Ede
Oregon State University

Paul Heilker
*Virginia Polytechnic Institute
and State University*

Peggy O'Neill
Loyola College

Victor Villanueva
Washington State University

SUBSCRIPTIONS

Composition Studies is published twice each year (May and November). Annual subscription rates: Individuals $25 (Domestic), $30 (International), and $15 (Students). To access a subscription form, please visit http://www.uc.edu/journals/composition-studies/subscriptions.html

BACK ISSUES

Some back issues from volume 13.1 and forward are available at $8 per issue. Photocopies of earlier issues are available for $3. To order or inquire about availability, see http://www.uc.edu/journals/composition-studies/subscriptions.html. More recent back issues are now available through Amazon.com. To find issues, use the advanced search feature and search on "Composition Studies" (title) and "Parlor Press" (publisher).

BOOK REVIEWS

Assignments are made from a file of potential book reviewers. To have your name added to the file, send a current vita to the Book Review Editor at ainoue@csufresno.edu.

JOURNAL SCOPE

The oldest independent periodical in the field, *Composition Studies* publishes original articles relevant to rhetoric and composition, including those that address teaching college writing; theorizing rhetoric and composing; administering writing programs; and, among other topics, preparing the field's future teacher-scholars. All perspectives and topics of general interest to the profession are welcome. We also publish Course Designs, which contextualize, theorize, and reflect on the content and pedagogy of a course. Contributions to Composing With are invited by the editor, though queries are welcome (send to compstudies@uc.edu). Cfps, announcements, and letters to the editor are most welcome. Composition Studies does not consider previously published manuscripts, unrevised conference papers, or unrevised dissertation chapters.

SUBMISSIONS

For submission information and guidelines, see http://www.uc.edu/journals/composition-studies/submissions/overview.html.

Direct all correspondence to:

>   Laura Micciche, Editor
>   Department of English
>   University of Cincinnati
>   PO Box 210069
>   Cincinnati, OH 45221–0069
>   compstudies@uc.edu

Composition Studies is grateful for the support of the University of Cincinnati.

©2013 by Laura Micciche, Editor
Production and printing is managed by Parlor Press, www.parlorpress.com.
ISSN 1534–9322

http://www.uc.edu/journals/composition-studies.html

composition STUDIES

Volume 41, Number 2
Fall 2013

From the Editor   9

Composing With

Revising a (Writer's) Life: Writing with Disability   12
    Michelle Gibson

Articles

ESL Droids: Teacher Training and the Americanization
Movement, 1919–1924   15
    Brian Ray

The Mediation of Literacy Education and Correspondence
Composition Courses at UNC–Chapel Hill, 1912–1924   40
    Courtney Adams Wooten

Course Designs

English 341: Advanced Composition for Teachers   58
    William Duffy

English 3135: Visual Rhetoric   78
    Oriana Gatta

Reviews

Writing Studies Research in Practice: Methods and Methodologies,
edited by Lee Nickoson and Mary P. Sheridan   99
    Reviewed by Amanda Athon

*New Natures: Joining Environmental History with Science and
Technology Studies,* edited by Dolly Jørgensen,
Finn Arne Jørgensen, and Sara B. Pritchard   103
    Reviewed by Danielle Hartke

Multimodal Literacies and Emerging Genres, edited by Tracey Bowen
and Carl Whithaus   107
    Reviewed by Michael Madson

Experimental Writing in Composition: Aesthetics and Pedagogies,
by Patricia Suzanne Sullivan   111
   Reviewed by Dan Martin

Thomas De Quincey: British Rhetoric's Romantic Turn,
by Lois Peters Agnew   115
   Reviewed by Patricia Mellon Moore

The Online Writing Conference: A Guide for Teachers and Tutors,
by Beth L. Hewett   119
   Reviewed by Sushil K. Oswal

A Synthesis of Qualitative Studies of Writing Center Tutoring 1983–2006, by Rebecca Day Babcock, Kellye Manning, Travis Rogers, and Courtney Goff   123
   Reviewed by Martha Wilson Schaffer

Evolutionary Rhetoric: Sex, Science, and Free Love in Nineteenth-Century Feminism, by Wendy Hayden   127
   Reviewed by Jacqueline Schiappa

Understanding the Essay, edited by Patricia Foster and Jeff Porter   131
   Reviewed by Madeline Walker

The WPA Outcomes Statement: A Decade Later, edited by Nicholas N. Behm, Gregory R. Glau, Deborah H. Holdstein, Duane Roen, and Edward M. White   134
   Reviewed by Courtney Adams Wooten

Announcements   138

Contributors   140

From the Editor

This journal began four decades ago as an 8.5 x 11" newsletter called *Freshman English News* (*FEN*). The first issue appeared in March 1972 as a "report on the status of Freshman English throughout the country" (1) that included sections on both four-year and two-year colleges. The practical focus on how writing and rhetoric were being taught across the U.S. stands in stark contrast to what was left out: "Theoretical and speculative articles should not be submitted" (3).

Reading through the first issue of *FEN* inspired that "everything old is new again" commonplace. For example, Richard Larson comments on diverse writing forms as central to "what we once knew as 'Freshman English,'" underscoring the perpetual instability of composition courses. In addition to studying literature, he argues, "freshman English, like possibly no other part of the curriculum in English," should also include "the study of all modes of communication, print, non-print verbal, and non-verbal" (1). His comment telegraphs the current focus on multimodality, visual and embodied rhetorics, and digital media in writing and rhetoric courses: *all modes of communication.*

I'm also struck by what's just plain old. An annual subscription was $2.00, for which one received several stapled, photocopied pages with content arranged in a single-sided three-column layout.

Not a single woman wrote for that first issue. Even the reviews are written by men on books published by men. Jim Corder contributes a column called simply "I Like These," in which he lists eleven recommended readings, not one written by a woman. Textbook advertisements for new books, some of which are authored or co-authored by women, are the only exception.

This glimpse into a disappointing (not really surprising) past is part of the journal's story. That story writ large is embodied in the archive that now fills an entire six-shelf bookcase in my office. I like the camaraderie of all those voices and words physically taking up space around me. With this first issue under my editorship going to press, I'm already aware of editorial work as a powerful form of curatorship, an opportunity to sponsor others' words, views, and distinctive registers. I would like to receive more submissions representing the diversity of our field, to interpret curatorship as a form of scholarly activism. I would like to reach more members of our field whose voices, experiences, and knowledge-making practices aren't yet represented adequately or at all.

When a (nonacademic) friend learned that I would be editing a journal called *Composition Studies*, he asked if it featured studies of how things are made. That is, he zeroed in on *composition* as the main thing. I'm trying to follow that impulse through the creation of the "Composing With" section, designed to showcase both "how things are made" and to acknowledge that making is always making *with*. For our very first contributor to this section, Michelle Gibson, composing with chronic illness ends up requiring her to re-learn how to write. Describing this learning process in terms of radical revision, Gibson eloquently writes, "I have been forced to revise long-held beliefs and habitual ways of functioning as a writer." I hope to run at least one piece in this section per issue. I want to insert composing and composition into a broad framework, placing writing alongside other art- and meaning-making activities, and represent diverse composing practices and partners.

This issue, shorter than subsequent ones due to the journal's transition from the University of Winnipeg to the University of Cincinnati, features two articles that take an historical approach to different aspects of teaching practices in 1920s American culture. Together, these articles produce a varied portrait of unconventional sites of literacy instruction. Brian Ray examines the Americanization Movement's effects on teacher training for student immigrant populations, and Courtney Adams Wooten connects early correspondence courses to contemporary distance education initiatives, identifying difficulties associated with both. Also included in this issue are two course designs: one on visual rhetorics, and the other on an advanced composition course for pre-service teachers. Finally, our book reviews cover a wide spectrum of new work on literacy, rhetoric, writing practices, situated writing initiatives, and more. I hope you'll discover new texts here that inspire and enlarge your perspective.

I want to take this opportunity to thank Jennifer Clary-Lemon, former editor of *Composition Studies*, for walking me through the editorial and business processes and for her patience and good will, particularly when my university took longer than seemed reasonable to facilitate the transfer. Asao Inoue has stayed on as book review editor, for which I am grateful. We are introducing review essays as a regular feature beginning with the next issue. We also invite dialogic reviews by collaborative teams (for more on this and other journal information, visit our new website at http://www.uc.edu/journals/composition-studies.html). I'm also indebted to editorial assistants Christina LaVecchia and Janine Morris, who have enthusiastically embraced their roles and responsibilities, making the process communal and fun for me. My department chair Jay Twomey has offered valuable support to me as well; without a course release, I'm not sure how I would have managed to pull this off.

A final word about the re-design of the journal's cover. Though I couldn't quite put my idea into words, I wanted for the cover an image that personified the *OED* definition appearing in the dialogue bubble, specifically "The forming (of anything) by combination of various elements, parts, or ingredients; formation, constitution, construction, making up." In looking through drawings made by my nine-year-old son Giovanni, an avid illustrator, I found the cat-snake hybrid you see on the cover. The image struck me as an embodiment of precisely the kind of "making up" that I couldn't fully articulate. My husband Gary, a visual artist (as well as writer and teacher), put the pieces of the composition together, designing the text, image, and overall presentation. In addition to the homegrown collaboration, I love that the cover evokes imagination, interest, and curiosity—crucial resources for all modes of communication

L.M.
Cincinnati, OH
October 2013

Works Cited

Corder, Jim W. "I Like These." *Freshman English News* 1.1 (March 1972): 3.
Larson, Richard L. "Freshman English in the 1970's." *Freshman English News* 1.1 (March 1972): 1–2.

Composing With

Revising a (Writer's) Life: Writing with Disability

Michelle Gibson

For the first decade of my career at the University of Cincinnati I taught writing. During that time, I participated in a project that involved creating videos that would form the core of online writing and literature courses. The videos were made in a studio that was completely empty but for me and a white board. Because I had no students with whom to work, no matter how hard I tried to behave as I would in the classroom, I kept acting and speaking in ways that were absolutely counter to my pedagogical and personal style. I pointed at a blank whiteboard as I talked, lectured for long stretches, and read aloud from assigned texts. At one point, I suddenly began to channel a crotchety old biddy. In a cackling voice I had not used before and hope that I have not used since, I looked into the camera and commanded, "Revise, revise, revise." At the next taping, the producers allowed me to revise that moment out of the video, but I had already told my partner about it and the Revision Hag I created that day has since become a humorous part of our family lore.

I am sorry to say that in 2008 the Revision Hag took up permanent residence in my life. That year, I was diagnosed with multiple sclerosis (MS). Not long after my diagnosis it became clear that mine is a progressive form of the disease and that the progression of my symptoms is aggressive. In the intervening years, I have gone from full-time employment as an academic to retirement on disability. Before my disease began to progress, I was teaching, writing professional articles and books, interacting with colleagues, directing my department's undergraduate program, and beginning to take my place in college leadership. Now, I am confined to a wheelchair, unable to drive, and experiencing increasing difficulty performing simple tasks (bathing and working on the computer, for instance) that were once second nature to me. Though I resist her at every turn, the Revision Hag reminds me always that I am now significantly disabled and that I must revise my ways of functioning.

The Revision Hag also commands that I revise the pace and frequency of my writing. Though MS does not impair one's intellect, it can affect some areas of cognitive functioning, particularly verbal fluency, the speed at which a person can process information and respond to it, short term memory, and executive functioning (planning and prioritizing). Early on, my neurologist suggested that I undergo "baseline" neuropsychological testing to determine the cognitive impact of my disease; those initial tests revealed measurable deficits.

When I was retested a year later, the deficits had increased significantly. I was already becoming aware that I might not be able to return to work the next year, and that awareness only grew as time passed and I found myself unable to write, speak, and process information as quickly and confidently as teaching and other academic work would require.

Even in the slow pace of my life on disability, the Revision Hag can be a harsh taskmistress. Just when I revise my ways of moving from place to place, of navigating my computer, of reading (because I can no longer turn the pages in a book, all of my reading is done on a computer or tablet), and of writing, my symptoms progress and I hear that cackling voice commanding, "Revise, revise, revise." I have been forced to revise long-held beliefs and habitual ways of functioning as a writer. I have had to revise my physical practice of writing, the value I place on certain types of writing, and my ideas about the very purpose of writing. As most people do, I once wrote using a computer that I controlled with my hands. I thought of writing as a process that involved not only my brain but also my body, particularly my arms and hands.

Lately, though, my hands have weakened and become uncoordinated, so I have had to revise the very basic ways I write and interact with my computer. I now spend my days wearing a headphone that controls my computer through voice recognition software. Everything I once did with my hands—including writing—I now do with my voice. The voice recognition software I use (Dragon Naturally Speaking) is probably the most popular on the market and it is definitely the most popular among people I know with MS. Dragon is a powerful program that easily recognizes the speaker's voice and builds a profile that keeps track of the writer's commonly used words and phrases. I have said many times that I wish I had found Dragon before my hands and arms were disabled because it allows my voice to connect directly with the page. All my life I have found it difficult to transfer my thinking from my mind, through my body, and onto the page. With Dragon what's on my mind goes directly onto the page; I find that liberating. Also, one of the reasons I loved teaching was that when I was in the classroom both my body and my negative body image disappeared, and I was able to be in the present and enjoy the moment in ways I never could in other contexts. With Dragon I get some of the same feeling; writing with my voice helps me forget my disabled body, to feel that it disappears in the same way it did when I was in the classroom.

With much chagrin, I recall that I once denigrated personal blogs as a kind of vain "self-publishing." I even remember saying once that anyone (serious writer or not) could have a blog, and believing that most blogs lack substance and are full of sloppy writing. Now, blogging is one of the primary types of writing I do. I read several wonderful blogs and I have my own blog (http://profspazz.com/), which focuses on my experience as a lesbian with MS. I have a set of regular followers, some of whom I know and some of whom have come to my blog through Internet searches or because it was recommended to them. I value this type of writing in ways that I never dreamed I would, for the blog has become my primary intellectual and creative outlet, as well as a way for me to "contribute" to the world despite the isolation imposed by my disability.

The Revision Hag has also insisted that I change my ideas about the connections between writing and sociality. As I said, I am no longer able to drive, so despite the fact that I am not working and should have plenty of time to socialize, it is difficult for me to do so on a regular basis. What's more, when I spent my days at the university most of my social life revolved around work. My closest friends were my colleagues, and I experienced extraordinary joy and social fulfillment in my interactions with students. Now those people have to come to my house to see me, and the easy interactions that came naturally when we spent our days interacting professionally require a kind of planning and forethought that makes them less frequent than any of us would like. Though the visits are wonderful, I have of necessity developed a very different kind of daily social life. I belong to an online MS support group that does much to sustain me socially. Though members come together only virtually and because of our common illness, we form a kind of daily coffee klatch full of humor; we talk about the issues of the day and we share the ups and downs of our lives.

As someone who became disabled in middle age, I was in the midst of a fully developed life as a scholar, teacher, and writer, and I had never even considered the possibility that the course of that life would be forever altered by MS. Now, knowing that my friends and colleagues are busy doing the kind of work and enjoying the kinds of interactions I once did, I feel as out of my element in this quiet house as I felt in that studio years ago. The solitude, the slow pace of my days, and writing whatever I want without a deadline are still as foreign to me as was "teaching" in that empty studio. As I contemplate the changes in my life and consider the revisions I must make in order to continue functioning in ways that are somewhat fulfilling to me, I remember with renewed compassion students who responded with horror to my suggestions that they revise their theses or the format of their essays. I understand like never before that the Revision Hag's command to revise, revise, revise sometimes represents not only the reconsideration of a piece of writing, but also of ways of seeing and living in the world.

ESL Droids: Teacher Training and the Americanization Movement, 1919–1924

Brian Ray

Historians of ESL have tended to concentrate on higher education as the primary site of their research, alluding to immigration and Americanization yet ultimately regarding them as peripheral. This article situates the Americanization Movement within an existing scholarly framework with particular attention to how teachers were selected and trained for working with adult immigrant populations. Similar to many contingent faculty situations today, these teachers were trained to deliver content that was heavily prescribed by manuals and other training materials. Documents from the period collected at Harvard University's Monroe C. Gutman Library show that local, state, and federal agencies worked with normal schools and university extension programs to cultivate a body of teachers that effectively functioned as "comp droids," a term used by Joe Harris to describe a labor pool lacking the agency and professional investment of tenure-track faculty. Although material conditions of contingent faculty today differ from those of Americanization teachers, the term helps to articulate the relevance of this period for contemporary discussions about teacher agency and contingent labor.

The Americanization Movement is an important but under-studied period in the history of composition and language difference, especially regarding historical materials on teacher training and their implications for teacher agency in the twenty-first century. Beginning in 1919 with the Americanization Bill and tapering off in 1924, when the U.S. passed the National Origins Act imposing immigration quotas, many states launched teacher-training initiatives reliant on collaboration between secondary schools, university extension programs, normal schools, and industries. The discourse emerging from these collaborations scripted teachers primarily as deliverers, rather than innovators, of curricular content. Teachers were not trained to develop their own lesson plans or materials. In fact, they were implicitly discouraged from doing so. Although documents from the period espouse a rhetoric of professionalization, what belies them is a desire for droids, to use Joe Harris' term, that would perform much like today's software programs or smartphone applications.

Some training programs for teachers were designed to be completed relatively quickly, not only by career teachers but also by those who saw teaching as a means of fulfilling a patriotic duty or providing a service to their company—secretaries, lawyers, factory mechanics—and to those classified as housewives.[1] Although teaching materials were partly based on progressive theories of English language instruction at the time, they were heavily adapted for two main goals—the cultural assimilation or "Americanization" of immigrants, and their acquisition of the English language so far as it made them economically productive. This history examines archival materials[2] in order to illustrate how teachers were recruited, educated about methods of teaching immigrants, and certified. It also interprets these materials in relation to how Americanization organizers saw teacher agency in classroom settings.

Histories of linguistic diversity and English language teaching by Tony Silva, Ann Raimes, Diane Musumeci, Paul Matsuda, and A. P. R Howatt and H. G. Widdowson have focused largely on universities as the historical locations of second-language instruction, treating the Americanization movement largely in passing. Meanwhile, historical work by John Trimbur, Bruce Horner, and Robert Connors has focused largely on pre-twentieth century origins of linguistic purity in the U.S. Addressing the evolution of ESL instruction in universities, Matsuda has argued that "ESL did not receive much serious attention until the 1940s" (17), after the University of Michigan founded the English Language Institute in order to teach Spanish-speaking students, with largely political motives. As Matsuda states, "the threat of totalitarianism coming into Latin American countries made the teaching of English to people from those nations a matter of national security for the United States, especially given their geographic proximity" (17). The Americanization Movement served as a precursor to the emergence of ESL at universities, one girded by a similar agenda to protect American political, cultural, and economic values.

Amy Dayton-Wood provides the only article-length discussion of Americanization in rhetoric and composition, analyzing the nationalist and assimilationist aims in immigrant education textbooks. While Dayton-Wood emphasizes how these materials scripted immigrants as citizens-in-the-making, I read materials from this period for what they reveal about the training of teachers who served a role similar to comp droids, a class of teachers who "have few of the intellectual interests of the professoriate" and instead merely assign and grade papers (Harris 43). Although Harris is describing the conditions of graduate teaching assistants and other contingent faculty more than sixty years after Americanization ended, the term aptly characterizes what leaders of that movement wanted—teachers who delivered lessons and did not seek a great degree of agency.

As Sidney Dobrin argues in *Don't Call It That*, teacher training is a crucial site through which different theories of language and rhetoric compete, and where political and cultural agendas for education are determined. Dobrin resists the notion of teacher training as preparing instructors only for the most practical elements of course management. The daily choices teachers make determine which theories survive and which ones fade, and so their initiation must expose them to the theory-practice continuum and encourage their growth as teacher-scholars. Nonetheless, a discourse persists in which teachers' inexperience justifies the practice of prescribing content, which delays or occludes that development. For instance, Ronda Leathers Dively privileges the advantages of common syllabi for new instructors at Southern Illinois University Carbondale over possible disadvantages, asserting that "the turn toward standardization stands to more effectively support the numerous GTAs who begin the program with no experience and with undeveloped pedagogical inclinations" (2010). Dively does recognize the long-term benefits of allowing new instructors to negotiate their own best practices in light of theories and pedagogies in rhetoric and composition. However, the desire for consistency wins out. Teacher inexperience becomes a rationale for standardization, as Dively explains:

> Rather than having the new GTAs build a course in addition to managing all the other challenges of composition instruction (not to mention the challenges of the graduate courses they are taking), at least part of the work is already completed, and, thus, the threat of becoming overwhelmed or having to "shoot from the hip" in pulling the course together is lessened. (2010)

My point is not to call out the use of common syllabi at a particular university, but to illustrate the temptation of seeing standardization as a solution for inexperience, and thus potentially falling prey to what Duane Roen, Maureen Daly Goggin, and Jennifer Clary-Lemon identify as the functional approach to teacher training that is more concerned with what to do on Monday morning than the long-term evolution of teacher-scholars.

The Americanization Movement represents a particularly conservative manifestation of the need to standardize instruction and produce passive teachers. This article will first explain the historical context of the Americanization Movement, analyze influential teaching manuals of the period, and then present the content of several teacher-training seminars and institutes. I will close with a reflection on how second-language instruction and pedagogies of linguistic diversity may benefit from greater emphasis on historical and contemporary issues of teacher training as a site to work toward dynamic pedagogies regarding language difference.

My historical research draws on materials at the Monroe C. Gutman Library at Harvard University. The Gutman Library houses perhaps the most extensive collection of materials on teacher training from the nineteenth and twentieth centuries. In addition to numerous manuals and textbooks, the Gutman Library has gathered a large number of pamphlets and reports on state and federal efforts to train teachers for educating adult immigrants in English during the first quarter of the twentieth century. Given the heavy concentration of immigrants in urban northeastern areas, most archival materials describe Americanization and teacher-training initiatives in states including Massachusetts, Pennsylvania, Ohio, Michigan, and New York. Other regions of the U.S. outside the industrialized northeast may have approached Americanization and teacher training differently, given either smaller numbers of immigrants or different regions of origin. As the next section of this article shows, most immigrants to the American Northeast hailed from Eastern and Southern Europe. Anxiety among state and city leaders about cultural and political disintegration appear to have been especially strong in these northeastern states, and they also appear to have run the most active programs of teacher training and Americanization.

Americanization and the Need for Teachers

Americanization had been an ongoing endeavor since the early 1900s. However, attention to the training of teachers increased significantly after the end of World War I, when the U.S. government (as well as the general public) began to debate problems arising from large numbers of immigrants. In *Patriotic Pluralism*, Jeffrey Mirel provides a vivid portrait of immigration issues in the U.S. at the time, stating that "between 1911 and 1920 alone nearly 8.8 million immigrants entered the United States" (Mirel 17). This influx came from Eastern and Southern Europe, including Austria-Hungary (2.15 million), Italy (2.05 million), and Russia (1.6 million). More than three quarters of these immigrants settled in the Northeast, in cities such as New York, Chicago, Detroit, Cleveland, Pittsburgh, Philadelphia, and Boston.

These numbers translated into significant changes in American cultural and political dynamics. Mirel observes, "[a]s newcomers flooded America's industrial cities, urban leaders and local politicians found themselves quickly overwhelmed by a series of intractable, interlocking problems," including "a growing gulf between rich and poor, overcrowding and disease in vast and expanding slums, widespread political corruption, inadequate or incompetent public services, and rampant crime" (Mirel 18). Immigrants were not the only cause of these problems, of course. Yet they were "implicated in all these developments" (18) because they were the most visibly different and the easiest to blame.

Four major schools of thought drove public discourse on Americanizing immigrants. Ultimately, the fourth and most conservative group, known as ethnic nationalists or racial restrictionists, would come to dominate and all but shut down large-scale Americanization efforts in 1924 (Mirel 46). The other three groups encouraged immigration but held different principles for integrating newly arrived immigrants. The first camp required a complete assimilation of immigrants, as articulated by Theodore Roosevelt and, later, Woodrow Wilson. Roosevelt went so far as to proclaim that the government "must Americanize [immigrants] in every way, in speech, in political ideas and principles, and in their way of looking at the relations between church and state" (qtd. in Mirel 26). By contrast, cultural pluralists such as John Dewey insisted that "the way to deal with hyphenism . . . is to welcome it . . . so that it shall surrender into a common fund of wisdom and experience" (qtd. in Mirel 31). In *Democracy and Education*, Dewey advocated for a diverse curriculum that recognized the contributions of many cultures to the advancement of knowledge and society. A third group promoted amalgamation, reframing the "melting pot" metaphor as the creation of a new type of citizen that would transcend all ethnicities. Finally, the fourth and most conservative group rejected immigration altogether, on the grounds that the Anglo-Saxon or Nordic race was so superior that integration could only hamper American prosperity and productivity.

Most new immigrants did not speak English, which made communication between civic leaders, native-born Americans, and immigrants extremely difficult. The language barrier therefore became a central point in the discourse about immigration. Immigrants had to learn English in order for the nation to prosper. Granted, language and citizenship courses had been ongoing in urban areas such as Chicago, Cleveland, Detroit, and New York since the early 1900s, but they lacked a uniform theory or teaching philosophy, and many were simply haphazard efforts by elementary school teachers. Mirel refers to one study of sixty-six evening courses for adult immigrants, in which a range of age-inappropriate assignments included "a group of weary steel workers [given] the task of copying the sentences: 'I am a yellow bird. I can sing. I can fly. I can sing for you'" (72).

Although the first "Americanization Day," celebrated on July 4, 1915, led to the establishment of the National Americanization Committee later that year (Mirel 24), education did not become a concern at the national level until 1919 when Bill 17, known as the Americanization Bill, was proposed by Senator Hoke Smith and U.S. Representative William B. Blankhead and passed into law. The bill outlined the necessity of not only educating immigrants but also training teachers for the task.[3] A Senate hearing on the bill included commentary by the secretary of the interior that teaching immigrants to "speak, read, and write the English language," as well as educating them in "the fundamental principles of government and citizenship," demand special resources for "the training and preparation of teachers, supervisors, and directors" (3). The bill provided $5 million toward these purposes at the federal level and $250,000 for each state. The secretary described the bill as a vital complement to the Smith-Towner Bill, aiming at long-term engagement with illiteracy in the U.S.

The bill envisioned the creation of special schools "in which teachers will be trained in this particular art of teaching the English language, both to grown-ups and to children" (6). Over the next two years, a number of arguments would emerge from the Bureau of Education for the location of teacher training specifically at normal schools. The newly founded Americanization Division held a major conference in May 1918 titled "Community Americanization," the proceedings of which were printed and mailed to Americanization workers nationwide, which would have included members of the Young Men's Christian Association, Red Cross, Daughters of the American Revolution, and a range of community organizations devoted to helping immigrants acclimate to American culture and civic life.

According to the 1919 hearing on the Americanization Bill, the Americanization Division formed two committees at the conference for "teaching English to a non-English speaking person and of deciding upon the fundamental principles underlying such a process" (59). State departments of education collaborated with university extension programs, normal schools, and large companies in the education of immigrants as well as the training of teachers. They offered materials, courses, and institutes for teachers. They were tested and licensed based on their ability to replicate what they learned from lectures and observations, rather than their ability to develop or implement their own pedagogies. In fact, in many cases the manuals and institutes were designed in such a way that non-career teachers, including clerks and foremen, could deliver the lessons with relatively minimal effort.

Despite this brief surge in attention, the Americanization Movement began to decline a few years later, when ethnic conservativism came to dominate public discourse. Bolstered by widespread fears of a socialist takeover following the 1917 Bolshevik Revolution, a rising tide of political and ethnic nationalism culminated in the passing of the National Origins Act in 1924. The 1924 act relied on the 1890 U.S. Census to construct a baseline for future immigration quotas, restricting the number of new immigrants to two percent of the foreign-born population of each nationality in the U.S that year. The act greatly reduced immigrant flows from Southern and Eastern Europe (Cannato, ch. 16). After the 1924 act was passed, the quota for Italians fell from approximately 40,000 a year to under 4,000; Russians from about 34,000 to about 2,000; and Greeks from about 3,000 to about 100 (ch. 16). The total number of immigrants allowed into the U.S. under the 1924 law fell to 164,000, and in 1927 the U.S. reduced that number further to 150,000. With fewer immigrants from Southern and Eastern Europe, the need for assimilation and language instruction became less compelling.[4] Although a small number of courses continued, public attention to Americanization and teacher training had faded by the end of the decade.

Teaching Manuals, Methods, and Agency

For a short time, the Americanization Movement witnessed a significant increase in attention to educating adult immigrants in English and produced a body of textbooks and manuals on teacher training. These documents reveal an orientation to teachers' professionalization that anticipates a recurring tension between the need for standardization and the need for agency. Although not mutually exclusive, these two have often pulled teachers and administrators in different directions, as illustrated in David Fleming's recent history on GTAs' resistance to common syllabi and standardized curricula at the University of Wisconsin–Madison in the 1960s, which led to conflicts with faculty and administration and, finally, the abolition of the university's first-year writing requirement in 1969. Much like the situation Fleming describes, the training manuals and textbooks used during the years 1919–1924 demonstrate a continued expectation that teachers deliver standardized instructional materials.

By 1920, several teacher-training manuals in immigrant education were in circulation. Although the manuals drew on then-progressive theories of language acquisition, they nonetheless prescribed nearly every aspect of instruction and left little room for experimentation. The manuals were written by a handful of recognized experts on immigrant education and language instruction including John J. Mahoney, Peter Roberts, and Henry Goldberger. These experts were actively involved in the day-to-day running of Americanization councils and teacher-training programs. Mahoney served as supervisor of Americanization in Massachusetts, Goldberger as a professor at the Columbia University Teachers College, and Roberts as immigration secretary of the International YMCA.

Mahoney, Roberts, and Goldberger played central roles in the development of teacher-training materials used throughout the Northeast. The Director of Americanization at the Bureau of Education, Fred Clayton Butler, intended books by these authors to "be available for the instruction of classes in the normal schools and colleges and for the actual use of teachers in their work with the foreign born" (United States, Committee on Education and Labor 59). According to a report by Charles Towne to the Massachusetts State Board of Education, Mahoney and Goldberger were especially active in the training of teachers in Massachusetts and New York. Goldberger also designed instructional pamphlets and three-year syllabi for teachers of immigrants in Pennsylvania, and Roberts' Direct Method was the model for teachers-in-training throughout Ohio. Moreover, a 1919 report by Don Lescohier, from the Extension Division of the University of Wisconsin, describes the content of a ten-week teacher-training course based on Roberts' and Goldberger's methods. Such reports suggest that Americanization and teacher-training efforts across the U.S. were following curricula outlined by these key figures.

Many of the manuals identify a need for special training to teach adult immigrants, but then dictate all aspects of the curriculum to such an extent that teacher agency to engage in independent research and contribute to a larger discourse is erased. In *Training Teachers for Americanization*, Mahoney situates the teaching of English to foreigners as a topic requiring unique knowledge. As he writes, "[n]o longer is the schooling of the immigrant to be an overtime task performed by teachers with only a casual training. . . . There is a distinct pedagogy in this work with adult immigrants and a very distinct methodology. The teacher of the immigrant must be acquainted with these" (7–8). Mahoney goes on to note the role of normal schools in the education of immigrants, that "here and there, as at Los Angeles, normal schools offered work in immigrant instruction as part of the year's program" (8). In many cases, teachers completed semester-long courses and exams in order to qualify for altogether-different licenses and certificates beyond their usual certifications to work in public schools. As Mahoney concludes, "schooling of the immigrant is no 'side-show,' to be conducted as before the Great War, when any one could teach, and when almost any one did. It is a highly specialized piece of work, and must be handled accordingly" (11).

The manuals advocated a handful of methods seen as effective at the time, all of them requiring only a teacher's recitation of lesson plans scripted down to the sentence. The outline of a teacher-training course offered at the University of Pittsburgh in 1919 defines five main methods along this vein. The first and most central was referred to as the Gouin method, after its creator Francois Gouin, which consisted of "[a] series of related sentences on a single theme . . . developed and dramatized in the presence of the class. The pupils repeat the expressions, perform the acts and then read, write and memorize the sentences" (Berkey 2). As Jack Richards and Theodore Rodgers state in *Approaches and Methods in Language Teaching*, Gouin himself was a French educational reformer who wrote during the mid-nineteenth century, and his method concerned foreign language learning and acquisition in general rather than ESL, which did not emerge as a distinct theory or pedagogy until Charles Fries founded the English Language Institute at the University of Michigan in 1941.[5]

Gouin was especially critical of the grammar-translation method of foreign language instruction, and while his ideas eventually became popular, they took several years to catch on, given that he wrote "at a time when there was not sufficient organizational structure in the language teaching profession (i.e., in the form of professional associations, journals, and conferences) to enable new ideas to develop into an educational movement" (Richards and Rodgers, ch.

1).⁶ Gouin's method influenced reformers in France and Germany in the later nineteenth century. Gouin also influenced Lambert Sauveur, who established a language academy in Boston during the 1860s, as well as Maximilian Berlitz, who founded a school in Providence, Rhode Island in 1878. An English version of Gouin's book titled *The Art of Teaching and Studying Languages* was finally published by Scribner in 1892. Through his predecessors, and the spread of his ideas in U.S., Gouin's method also became known as the Direct Method, which stressed using the target language in the classroom, as opposed to analysis and memorization of grammatical rules (Richards and Rodgers, ch. 1).

Gouin's method is important because it formed the basis of the most prominent textbooks and manuals designed for teaching English to adult immigrants in the U.S. In fact the second-most-popular method, the Roberts or YMCA Method⁷, is described as "a type of the Gouin Method," and it stressed that "New English words must first be taught through the ear and then reproduced orally by the pupils before the eye and the hand are enlisted in learning" (Berkey 2). According to the Roberts Method, "[a] new language is learned only through its intelligent use by the pupils and in its simple expression of their daily experiences and common interests," and "[a]ll lessons in English must follow the natural law of related thinking and logical development" (2). In the preface to the teaching manual *English for Coming Americans*, Roberts directly admits that Gouin's book "furnished me with the basic idea which is worked out herein" (Roberts 5). The third method was referred to as the Ford-DeWitt Method, a "modification of the Roberts Method [which was implemented at the Ford factory in Michigan and] designed to introduce the vocabulary of words and sentences of special value to the workers in a factory" (Berkey 2). Itself essentially a derivation of Gouin's approach, the Ford-DeWitt method became a model for other factories across the industrialized Northeast.

The fourth method, the Berlitz Method, was conducted through a series of readings in which "teachers ask questions to be answered by the pupils in the words of the text. The new language is thus taught largely by conversation" (2). According to Richards and Rodgers, Berlitz did not create a new method so much as adapt Gouin's method, without direct acknowledgement of Gouin's work (Richards and Rodgers, ch. 1). Finally, the Word and Sentence Method consisted of "teaching the forms and the meaning of a number of words as the basal vocabulary from which short sentences are constructed. . .essentially the 'see and say' method of primary grade schools" (Berkey 2). The first four methods, all variations of Gouin's, were dominant in the Americanization Movement, especially as state departments of education, university extension programs, normal schools, and various industries used them in their collaborations to train immigrant factory workers.

Henry Goldberger's *Teaching English to the Foreign Born* accurately represents teacher manuals from this period, especially the desire to regulate and standardize instruction down to the level of spoken sentences and their accompanying gestures. Goldberger was influential in the Americanization Movement, teaching courses at the Teachers College while helping develop manuals and materials for other states such as Pennsylvania, Ohio, Cleveland, Illinois, and Massachusetts. Goldberger resisted earlier approaches to immigrant education, instead embracing the Gouin or "theme method," which introduced learners to sets of related sentences that referred to their immediate environment.

Appropriating Gouin's method for work with adult immigrants learning English, Goldberger argued that "the foreign born desires to be taught such English as he can use at once in the world outside of the classroom" (11). Such situations included letter writing, road sign reading, dances, card games, sports games, business investments, doctor appointments, and work. Goldberger encouraged teachers to adopt settings and attitudes similar to those in social clubs, where immigrants learned English from conversation rather than rote exercises.

Goldberger's manual promoted a progressive theory of language acquisition for its time. However, it assumed teachers' lack of skill or preparation and so over-determined the content, timing, and sequencing of exercises. In essence, Goldberger boiled down Gouin's 440-page treatise on language teaching into a series of easily replicable lessons constructed around sets of sentences such as "I walk to the door" and "I turn the knob" (15). The teacher was directed to illustrate the lessons through active body language. The book insisted that "[t]he sentences must be short and so worded that the meaning of each and every part of each sentence may be made clear to the foreign born by means of action, dramatizations, and by the use of objects or pictures" (15). Additionally, teachers were instructed to use no more than ten sentences, all related by "sequence or by cause and effect," per lesson (15).

The third and longest chapter of Goldberger's manual outlined ten daily lesson plans using this model, and provided a detailed chart showing how much time teachers should spend on conversation, word drills, sentence drills, writing, and reading (21). A typical lesson consisted of eight separate steps that instructors were to act out for the class. First, instructors would stand before the class and say, "I shut my eyes," as they performed the sentence by shutting their eyes. Next they would open their eyes and say, "I open my eyes." The third step directed instructors to allow the class to practice. Instructors would then write the sentence on the board for students to sound out to themselves, even if they lacked knowledge of the alphabet. Only near the end of the ten units did the manual encourage teachers to "adjust [their] teaching to meet [pupils'] ever present needs," especially the "technical expressions" that immigrants use at work (35).

In an earlier manual titled *English For Coming Americans*, Peter Roberts lays out a nearly identical plan, drawing on Gouin's methods to critique foreign language instruction based on the analysis of grammar and the translation of literary passages. Roberts even shares an anecdote about "a gentlemen who, having taught German for many years in one of our colleges, was ludicrously put out of countenance when in his travels he tried to talk that language" (12). Similar to Goldberger, Roberts mandates a rigid system of thirty lessons, each consisting of roughly a dozen sentences organized around a particular activity like waking up and getting dressed, clocking in at work, going to the bank, or mailing a letter. In a subsequent manual titled *English for Foreigners*, Roberts explains this method in detail for members of the coal-mining industry in Illinois, which had a large population of Eastern and Southern European immigrants like much of the urban Northeast.

Roberts' sentence sequences revolved around immigrants' domestic, industrial, and commercial lives and included lessons on preparing breakfast (domestic), dealing with accidents and injuries (industrial), and making bank deposits (commercial). Roberts illustrates the method with a lesson on waking up, in which teachers repeated and dramatized phrases like "I get out of bed" and "I comb my hair." He encourages teachers to use props for sequences that involve objects like combs or kitchen utensils. Each lesson follows a rigid three-step sequence. In the first step, the teacher repeats every sentence multiple times until students can rehearse the entire series by themselves. Next "the teacher should hang up a chart on which is printed the lesson and the class see the words for the first time" before they "read the lesson in concert" (43). After repeating this step "three or four times," the teacher then distributes paper to the students for them to practice copying the lesson while the teacher passes "from student to student, correcting and suggesting improvement" (43). Even the fourth review stage is heavily scripted, instructing the teacher to cover up all of the sentences with newspaper except for the verbs, which are to provide catalysts for students to recite the entire series over again. Finally, teachers lead practical instruction in grammar, having students replace personal pronouns like "I" with "you," and so on (44).

There can be no deviation from these steps, and Roberts further requires teachers to review lessons in a rigid schedule, maintaining that "time should be taken in each session for review of the lesson given two nights previous" (44). For example, "[w]hen the third lesson is being taught, the first should be reviewed; when the fourth is being taught the second should be reviewed, etc" (44). Teachers only prepared by memorizing and practicing these sequences in order to appear confident before their students. Nothing in the Roberts Method discusses the creation of lesson plans, exercises, or sequences other than those narrated in extreme detail. Although such methods may have helped ensure consistency via simplicity and specificity, by today's standards they hardly seem like actual teaching.

Most manuals expected teachers to plan for each lesson by carefully studying and rehearsing the lessons on their own time. As Roberts states in another manual titled *The Problem of Americanization*, teachers should "be a master in each lesson, appear before the class confident that you can give it knowledge, so that if unexpected difficulties arise you will not be disconcerted" (85). A prepared teacher was one who memorized his or her part and performed like a well-oiled machine. Like Roberts and Goldberger, moreover, Mahoney limited instruction to sentences and phrases that would help immigrants become better workers or better citizens. As Mahoney states, "Rather than teach a carpenter the English that goes with laying bricks, the teacher must plan the lesson to be of value to the carpenter. It is better for the pupil to understand the signs posted in his factory than the signs in any other factory" (35). Mahoney's manual then provides a few brief examples of phrases and words about industrial safety, searching for work, and payday.

At best, the materials on teacher training are unclear about working conditions and salaries for teachers. Reports on Americanization efforts do not typically provide information on teacher compensation, and training manuals themselves often gloss over the issue by evoking a spirit of patriotism and self-sacrifice, which may suggest teachers were not paid all that well. A 1920 report by the Special Commission on Teacher Salaries in Massachusetts verifies that while teachers' salaries did improve significantly from 1910 to 1920, they were "not equivalent to the increase in cost of living" (27). High school teachers' salaries grew by 50.7%, but cost of living almost doubled, rising by 99.7% (25). In terms of a dollar amount, high school teachers made, on average, $1,164.67 annually in 1910, compared to $1,695.48 in 1920. (Elementary school teachers earned less.) By contrast, the cost of living in Massachusetts in 1920 was estimated at roughly $1,100 a year (23). This figure included only the most basic necessities of food, clothing, shelter, fuel, and "sundries."

Moreover, the Massachusetts special report in 1920 states that 70% of teachers often paid out of pocket for their own development such as "professional improvement courses, tuition, books, etc," and that 40% of teachers did so for "[a]ttendance at summer schools," which would have included training courses and seminars discussed later in this article. This may explain why some manuals touted a sense of self-sacrifice. For instance, according to Roberts, "[t]he work is not to be measured by the number of kilograms of energy [the teacher] loses, but by the molding of men and women into good American citizens" (103). Roberts went so far as to praise teachers who worked without a wage, proclaiming that "[s]ome of the best men I have seen in the work were not paid a cent. Rain or snow, frost or blizzard could not keep them away from their classes. . . . We need the spirit of self-sacrifice in the work" (103). It is difficult not to see these statements as attempts to redirect teachers toward self-satisfaction, and therefore away from thoughts about material conditions.

Teacher-Training Courses

Historical documents show that while some training programs were selective, in other cases almost anyone could and did complete short courses that led to certification to teach English in a range of non-institutional settings such as factories, social clubs, civic centers, and private homes. This section as well as the next details who could become a teacher and what requirements they had to complete. Although Mahoney had predicted the professionalization of immigrant education, it did not necessarily lead to greater agency for teachers—most likely because of the prescriptive tone of the manuals as well as an openness to training anyone at all to teach English to immigrants.

Teacher training courses in Pennsylvania, Illinois, Massachusetts, Wisconsin, Ohio, and New York, among other places, were designed and implemented by state boards of education in cooperation with normal schools and university extension programs. According to a 1921 report from the Massachusetts Department of Education, between 1918 and 1919 more than a dozen normal schools in the state certified 1,300 people (mostly public school teachers) to teach English to immigrants. Some were career teachers while others were clerks, librarians, lawyers, ministers, housewives, or typists. These courses not only trained teachers in methods of language instruction but also the perceived importance of promoting assimilation to American values, civic virtues, and social integration. In many of these courses, teachers were encouraged to develop and nurture partnerships between social clubs and organizations, community centers, libraries, factories, and schools. The courses trained teachers as well as community organizers and administrators, sometimes splitting classrooms into different groups for tailored topics.

In some cases, training was a highly selective process. A 1919 report stated that Pittsburgh University planned to offer a two-week summer institute as well as a six-week "intensive training course" that "consists of 24 lessons of two hours each" and required teachers-in-training "to make two visits to evening schools and write a thesis" ("Americanization Work in Pittsburgh" 5). Admission was competitive, as the report states that students had to be approved for enrollment by the Frick Educational Commission, which funded the course. The report states that 184 teachers had enrolled in its training courses up to that point. Even after completing the training, however, teachers still had to be elected by the School Board after receiving a recommendation from the Superintendent of Schools (3).

A report on Americanization work in New York also describes rigorous teacher-training courses, the main goal of which was to "develop competent teachers to give immigrant instruction in the English language and to familiarize him with American customs, laws and standards of living" (9). Completion of the course required "a carefully prepared note book containing notes on all the lectures given at the institution" that "must be submitted for examination at the end of the course"; "[b]ook reviews as assigned by the local director"; "[a] paper which indicates definite research and original thought"; and finally "[a] final examination which will be a real test of the main lines of thought presented at the institute" (13). Prospective teachers were also heavily encouraged to visit factory and neighborhood classes to observe and take notes.

A brochure printed by the State University of New York in 1920 advertised a six-week, thirty-hour "Summer Course for Teacher Training" on Americanization and citizenship, organized by the university "in cooperation with colleges, universities, normal schools and other educational agencies in the state." The course devoted attention to English teaching for the foreign-born in the last of three sections. The previous two sections were devoted to surveys of immigration and methods for teaching civics. The brochure stated that the class sessions were "supplemented by required readings, special papers, note books, and final examination" (3). Successful completion of the course earned the newly trained teachers a state certificate. Faculty included professors from the New York State College for Teachers, Adelphi College, Teachers College and Hunter College, and Cornell University.

Content in these courses covered not only methods for teaching English to foreigners, but also political and socio-economic factors of immigration and the need to assimilate them. In addition to topics in "Methods of Teaching English to Foreigners," teachers also had to learn "State and Federal Plans for Americanization" as well as "Economic Aspects of Immigration and Their Interpretation" (9). Dozens of colleges and institutions collaborated in offering these courses, including professors from The State College for Teachers in Albany and members of the Council for Women's Organizations—and even neighborhood associations. The State University of New York certified teachers upon completion, and it was assured that "[s]chool authorities will give preference to those holding this certificate when considering applications for work with foreign-born adults" (13).

Teachers were expected to demonstrate thorough knowledge in principles of Americanization and assimilation. As a final exam given by the Teachers College of the University of Cincinnati shows, they had to explain methods of language instruction as well as the socio-political implications of their work:

Questions:

1. Define Americanization—What it is and what it seeks to accomplish.
2. Indicate some fundamental principles which should determine the course content in civics and community life for immigrants.
3. Give a brief outline of the direct method of teaching English to immigrants.
4. What characteristics and education should a social worker and teacher among immigrants have?
5. Does the United States need immigrant labor? Why?
6. What social problems are involved in Americanizing immigrants in Cincinnati?
7. What part do you think the public schools and their teachers have in Americanization in Cincinnati?
8. Give a brief statement of any one of the problems which immigrants create in our city and constructive and practical solution thereof.
9. What results can be expected through the establishment of the American House?
10. What suggestions have you to offer as to a program of activities for this enterprise? Localize and make your suggestions concrete. (Eisler 3)

The most thorough account of teacher training is given in a report by the Massachusetts State Department of Education in September 1920. The report provides a detailed syllabus for a summer course offered at the State Normal School at Hyannis. (A 1926 report by the Massachusetts State Board of Education describes the course as being offered every summer since 1920, as well as a similar summer course at the North Adams Normal School.) Two versions of the courses were offered: one for supervisors and organizers (see Figure 1), a second for teachers (see Figure 2). The teacher-training courses were offered free of charge by the state of Massachusetts to all residents, with the exception of a $35 boarding fee, which provided attendees with lodging at the normal school. The curriculum for both versions of the course is outlined in Figures 1 and 2.

Faculty for these courses included officials from the state board of education: Charles Towne, former superintendent of education reform; Charles Herlihy, assistant superintendent of schools; Mary Guyton, assistant to the state supervisor; Philip Davis, a lecturer on immigrant education from Boston University; John J. Mahoney, state supervisor of Americanization; Denis McCarthy, poet-lecturer; George Tupper, secretary of the state executive committee of the YMCA; and M. J. Downey, director of Americanization for the city of Boston. As with the manuals, consistency and replicability constituted the rhetoric of these teacher-training courses. Teachers were measured mainly by their abilities to adopt and transmit ready-made materials.

Course I.
For Supervisors and Organizers of Americanization Activities.
(Open only to people who have had some experience in Americanization work.)

    A. Americanism and Americanization.
        1. Americanism—an analysis.
        2. Americanization—the broad interpretation.
        3. The function of the school.
        4. The immigrant tide.
        5. Legislation affecting immigration and Americanization.
        6. Beginning and development of Americanization movement.
        7. Industrial Americanization.
        8. Americanization and the immigrant woman.
    B. How to organize a community.
        1. A study of State and city plans.
        2. Securing the co-operation of industry.
        3. Organizing women's classes.
        4. The functions of various community agencies.
        5. The socialized school as a community center.
    C. Naturalization and citizenship.
        1. The content of a course in citizenship.
        2. Materials of instruction.
        3. The process of naturalization—problems and difficulties.
        4. Activities of the Federal Bureau of Naturalization.
    D. Racial backgrounds and characteristics.
        1. Type studies of a few prominent immigrant groups.
        2. Readings and discussions.

Figure 1.

Course II.
An Elementary Course for Teachers

    A. Americanism and Americanization.
       Content as indicated for Course I.
    B. Classroom work with the adult immigrant.
        1. Classifications of students.
        2. Aims for the several grades.
        3. The psychology underlying method of teaching English to immigrants.
        4. A comprehensive-direct method.
        5. Lesson context for the several grades.
        6. A study of texts and other sources.
        7. The socialized school.
    C. Naturalization and citizenship.
       Content as indicated for Course I.
    D. Racial backgrounds and characteristics.
       Content as indicated for Course I.

Figure 2.

A report by Charles Towne for the Department of University Extension in Massachusetts commented directly on the need to standardize instruction, admitting that he was "disappointed in the quality and type of teaching that I saw in most of the schools [when visiting Ohio]. Instead of clear, clean-cut application of the direct method [the Gouin or Roberts Method], I found an apparent confusion in the minds of the teachers as to just what method they ought to use and how it should be applied" (4). Towne went on to describe the overall lack of conformity in instructional materials and to criticize the director of the Cleveland program for not providing a standardized pamphlet or set of handouts for use in classrooms. Overall, the report appears displeased with the idea of teachers taking the development of materials into their own hands, rather than following a set of prescriptions handed down from a central administrator.

Industries sometimes provided the facilities for instruction, in order to encourage attendance by their workers. Once trained, some teachers taught in factories during immigrant workers' lunch breaks or immediately after their shifts. A 1922 report from the Massachusetts State Department of Education described the results of an important conference between "more than 300 industrial executives and school officials" who "reached an agreement through which to establish factory classes on a regular basis" (53). In the agreement, the factory would provide the facilities for onsite classrooms and contribute a supervisor to oversee the organization of classes and recruitment of students from their workers. The state would furnish everything else, including trained teachers. One of the best-known factory schools emerged at a cotton mill in Lowell, Massachusetts, where ten state-certified teachers were sent to conduct hour-long English classes during lunch and after workers' day shifts. According to the 1922 report, "The mill set off a large part of a supply room and made six class rooms, equipped with blackboards, tables, benches, and the like" (53). The curriculum seemed to consist largely of lessons and activities suited to the work itself, given that "[a] committee of plant officials and teachers devoted several weeks to the preparation of a series of lessons on the cotton industry. The purpose of such material was to help the alien learn the language of the shop and also to give him some insight into the different kinds of work done in the plant" (53). Such courses went on for three years, 1920–1923, resulting in 600 "alien men" graduating each spring. They were honored in an April graduation ceremony attended by teachers, school officials, and plant executives. The report indicates that more than 300 other types of factory classes were offered throughout the state during the year 1923 alone, educating 4,000 factory workers.

Here the relationship between governments, universities, and industry becomes especially apparent. State governments certified teachers educated through extension programs and normal schools, in many cases so that they could deliver a pre-fabricated curriculum for the sake of producing more efficient workers. Of course, in some cases states permitted industries to train and certify their own factory workers as teachers. The next section explores in further detail how non-career teachers often took on the work of instruction and became "trained" in immigrant education.

Training Teachers (and Anybody Else)

If immigration posed a threat to civic unity and economic productivity, it also presented a need for an efficient mechanism that could churn out teachers. The Bureau of Education began to cooperate with city and state governments in offering teacher-training courses to public school teachers as well as a range of workers in other professions. English for Immigrants appeared to require a special method of instruction, but that method could be completely scripted, standardized, and imparted to anyone regardless of their prior knowledge or training in the field of education. A 1919 report by the Massachusetts State Board of Education describes the development of a sixty-lesson plan designed in an effort to standardize instruction, because "this branch of education is still so uncertain in its methods and standards" that "any teachers must of necessity be relatively untrained and in need of the right kind of teaching material" (144). The "right kind of material" was intended to be simple and easy to deliver, making the presence of a career-teacher optional.

Anyone could teach immigrants English, or so the logic of teacher-training programs suggested. The same 1919 report from the Massachusetts State Department of Education identified criteria for potential teachers as the "ability to speak and understand English," "[i]ntelligent devotion to American ideals," "understanding and sympathetic appreciation of the immigrant," and a "personality adapted to this kind of teaching" (138). Anyone with these qualities, even without training or experience, could enroll in a certification program and be teaching English to immigrants within a matter of weeks. Consistent with this view, a statement from the director of Americanization in Ohio lists enrollment by profession in a teacher-training course. In addition to fifty teachers enrolled at the Teacher's College in Cincinnati there were

   2 typists
   3 stenographers
   3 artists
   5 kindergarten teachers
   3 secretaries
   8 social workers
   7 housewives

4 no occupation
2 music teachers
2 attorneys
2 reporters
2 ministers
2 library clerks
2 bookkeepers
44 "of Indefinite Occupation."

Many of the teachers-in-training identified here appear to have no prior training. As such, they may have been viewed by city and state leaders as likely to accept the scripts carved out for them by the manuals and training institutes. Although normal schools offered semester-long courses in immigrant education, a non-career teacher could achieve certification through the state by attending ten class meetings, submitting a notebook "given in class" along with a 1,000-word book review, and a 1,000-word thesis on an assigned topic. The state of Massachusetts kept "[a]n approved list of teachers. . .in the office of the department," and "[s]pecial certificates" were "awarded to foremen and other employees who take the short course in methods for the purpose of teaching in the plant where they are employed" (138–39).

A report by Howard C. Hill to the American Council on Education describes such non-specialists as trained and employed by the Ford Motor Company's Ford English School in Detroit. Located on site and consisting of twenty-eight specially designed classrooms, the school offered teacher-training courses every Wednesday. Classes for immigrants were normally offered at 8 a.m., 1 p.m., and 3:30 p.m., before or after their eight-hour shifts. However, all of Wednesday was blocked out for teacher training. Teachers were recruited from across the company and included secretaries as well as factory workers. They were not paid for either the training or teaching. According to the report,

> The teachers are volunteers from the employees of the factory itself. They represent clerks, foremen, checkers, inspectors, stenographers, machinists, and eight other classes of workers. Here you find in actual operation the American employee teaching English on his own time, because he wants to be of service to the foreigner. There seems to be something in this spirit of unselfish service that appeals to foreign and native mind alike. (2)

The language used in the report on the Ford English School devalues teaching as a specialized profession, in the name of economic expediency couched in the language of selflessness and love of company. It suggests that some companies believed they could train teachers as well as, if not better than, their counterparts in the school system—and that the main criteria for certifying a teacher was an interest in serving fellow workers. Factories across the northeast were mainly interested in teaching the English needed to operate equipment efficiently and safely, although they also stressed naturalization, assimilation, and civic virtue as secondary goals of language instruction. Jeffrey Mirel describes the Ford Motor Company as particularly draconian in this regard. Ford laid off immigrant employees if they did not attend the onsite English school, and in 1914 the company fired 900 Greek and Russian workers for staying home to observe Eastern Orthodox Christmas, two weeks after December 25, on the reasoning that immigrants should only observe "American" holidays (83).

Making Pasts Visible

A more in-depth understanding of Americanization as a precursor to present-day debates on teacher training and language difference in higher education serves a number of purposes. First, it helps articulate the ever-present need to remain mindful of language education's imbrications with political and corporate agendas. Scott Wible has observed "the potential for government funding to alter the infrastructure and influence the responsibilities of U.S. language arts education" (472). As a government-sponsored endeavor, the Americanization Movement united universities, normal schools, departments of education, and industries in the purpose of engineering a program of teacher indoctrination meant to distribute uniform content. This discourse resulted in a predetermined role for teachers as less active agents in the development of theories and pedagogies of adult language teaching than they could have been. In this regard, Americanization was not only a prelude to controversial issues of language policy and linguistic diversity, but also to debates about professionalization and material conditions. It is important to remain cautious of temptations to standardize instruction, therefore marginalizing linguistically diverse students and "relieving" inexperienced teachers of the need to develop their own practices based on independent explorations of scholarship. Although standardizing composition curricula may generate efficiency, it does so at the expense of the discipline's creative and intellectual dimensions.

The movement also has particular relevance for historical work on language difference and English language teaching. As Matsuda states, historical inquiry "can contribute insights into the socially shared and discursively constructed identity of the field and its members" as well as "identify what issues have been discussed, what questions have been posed, what solutions have been devised, and what consequences have come of those solutions—and why" (32). Margaret Thomas has critiqued second language theorists, who "consistently ignore the past as discontinuous with the present" and so "make the past invisible" (qtd. in Matsuda 34). Such histories and critiques of dominant discourse have sought to relocate historical considerations of ESL teaching from the margins of literature reviews and chronologies back to "the mainstream discourse of second language studies" (34).

This article has likewise sought to uncover problems, debates, solutions, and consequences of a prototype of ESL instruction that occurred *before* the 1940s and, in many cases, beyond the scope of the university. Many of these concerns are reflected in present-day shifts in education such as the increasing enrollment of international students at universities as well as the rise in alternative modes of education, including for-profit institutions, online education, and now Massively Open Online Courses (MOOCs). This article cannot go into depth on all of the ramifications of these changes, but it is my hope that readers will pursue connections between this particular moment in history and present-day challenges to the traditional structures of higher education. The challenges are prompting teachers, scholars, and administrators to look outside universities and adapt in ways that fulfill democratic and egalitarian purposes of education while remaining aware of competing agendas in higher education's past as well as its future.

Notes

1. Mention of this last group may sound ironic given that the nineteenth amendment, ensuring women's suffrage, was not passed until 1920, suggesting that while women were not trusted with the vote, they were seen as a potential labor pool for Americanization efforts.

2. I am thankful for the special collections librarians at Harvard University's Monroe C. Gutman Library, which houses an extensive collection of materials on the Americanization Movement. I am also thankful for the Research Services Council at the University of Nebraska at Kearney, which funded my travel to Harvard in early 2013.

3. The hearing on the Americanization Bill appealed heavily to values of patriotism and worker efficiency, citing statistics that three million immigrant farmers in 1918 could not read material the government had distributed about Liberty Bonds, the need to produce more wheat, and other national interests (6). A census cited in the Secretary of Interior's address introducing the bill states that 24% of soldiers in the armed forces did not know enough English to "sign pay rolls" or even "read the War Department's orders" (6).

4. Immigration numbers fell even further following the 1929 stock market crash, and rates remained low during the 1930s largely due to the Depression. According to Steven G. Darian in *English as a Foreign Language*, less than 350,000 Europeans immigrated to the U.S. from 1931 to 1940 (Darian 79).

5. Fries would turn away from all prior methods of foreign language instruction, advocating a unique theory and pedagogy of ESL in his book, *Teaching and Learn-*

ing English as a Foreign Language. Fries helped inaugurate the audio-lingual method of foreign language instruction, and it was used extensively in ESL instruction in universities. It still consisted of short oral dialogues and drills seemingly similar to the ones used by Americanization teachers. The difference is that audiolinguists organized their exercises around increasingly complex grammatical structures, for example having students repeat the same utterance multiple times while varying verb tense or pluralizing nouns. Gouin, and adaptors of his method, organized exercises around everyday themes, assuming that grammar would be absorbed naturally over time.

6. Before Gouin the grammar-translation method, defined as the analysis and memorization of a language's grammatical rules, dominated foreign language education in North American and European universities (Richards and Rodgers, ch. 1). Whereas the grammar-translation method was derived from the study of Latin in the Middle Ages, Gouin's method emphasized modern languages and oral communication in everyday situations. Gouin dismissed written exercises in grammar and translation as a means to teaching modern foreign languages. Instead, he advocated conversational activities that would help students in everyday personal, social, and civic contexts (basic friendly conversation and daily activities like cooking breakfast, chopping wood, and trips to the store). Many of the textbooks and manuals about teaching English to adult immigrants drew on Gouin's methods, as adapted by Henry Goldberger and Peter Roberts.

7. Roberts' teaching manual, *English for Coming Americans*, was published in 1909, almost a decade prior to the Americanization Bill. Nonetheless, Roberts was an influential figure well into the 1920s.

Works Cited

Berkey, J. M. Extracts from *Outlines of A Teacher-Training Course in Americanization and Citizenship*. Washington: GPO, 1918. TS. History of Education and Teacher Training Collection, Monroe C. Gutman Lib., Harvard U, Cambridge.

Cannato, Vincent. *American Passage: The History of Ellis Island*. New York: Harper Perennial, 2010. Kindle file.

Darian, Steven G. *English as a Foreign Language: History, Development, and Methods of Teaching*. Norman: U of Oklahoma P, 1972. Print.

Dively, Ronda Leathers. "Standardizing English 101 at Southern Illinois University Carbondale: Reflections on the Promise of Improved GTA Preparation and More Effective Writing Instruction." *Composition Forum* 22 (2010): n. pag. Web. 20 July. 2013.

Dobrin, Sydney. *Don't Call it That: The Composition Practicum*. Urbana, IL: NCTE, 2005. Print.

Ede, Lisa, and Andrea A. Lunsford, eds. *Selected Essays of Robert J. Connors*. New York: Bedford/St. Martin's, 2003. Print.

Eisler, George. *Statement of Director of Americanization Executive Committee, Cincinnati, OH, Regarding Institutes*. N.d. TS. History of Education and Teacher Training Collection, Monroe C. Gutman Lib., Harvard U, Cambridge.

Fleming, David. *From Form to Meaning: Freshmen Composition and the Long Sixties, 1957–1974*. Pittsburgh: U of Pittsburgh P, 2011. Print.

Fries, Charles C. *Teaching and Learning English as a Foreign Language*. Ann Arbor: U of Michigan P, 1945. Print.

Goldberger, Henry H. *Teaching English to the Foreign Born: A Teacher's Handbook*. Washington: GPO, 1920. TS. History of Education and Teacher Training Collection, Monroe C. Gutman Lib., Harvard U, Cambridge, MA.

Gouin, Francois. *The Art of Teaching and Studying Foreign Languages*. Trans. Howard Swan and Victor Betis. New York: Scribner, 1892. PDF file.

Harris, Joseph. "Meet the New Boss, Same as the Old Boss: Class Consciousness in Composition." *CCC* 52.1 (2000): 43–68. Print.

Hill, Howard C. *Industrial Americanization: Extracts from Report of Howard C. Hill to the American Council on Education: Covering the Sicher System, the Ford English School, and the Correspondence Courses of the Pennsylvania Railroad System*. Washington: GPO, 1918. TS. History of Education and Teacher Training Collection, Monroe C. Gutman Lib., Harvard U, Cambridge.

Horner, Bruce, and John Trimbur. "English Only and U.S. College Composition." *CCC* 53.4 (2002): 594–630. Print.

Howatt, A. P. R., and H. G. Widdowson. *A History of English Language Teaching*. Oxford: Oxford UP, 2004. Print.

Lescohier, Don D. *Statement Concerning 10 weeks' Course for Teachers of Immigrants at the University of Wisconsin*. Washington: GPO, 1919. TS. History of Education and Teacher Training Collection, Monroe C. Gutman Lib., Harvard U, Cambridge.

Mahoney, John J., Frances K. Wetmore, Helen Winkler, and Elsa Alsberg. *Training Teachers for Americanization: A Course of Study for Normal Schools and Teachers' Institutes*. Washington: GPO, 1920. Print.

Massachusetts Department of Education. *Annual Report of the Department of Education For the Year Ending November 30, 1919*. Boston: The Commonwealth of MA, 1920. TS. History of Education and Teacher Training Collection, Monroe C. Gutman Lib., Harvard U, Cambridge.

—. *Annual Report of the Department of Education For the Year Ending November 30, 1923*. Boston: The Commonwealth of MA, 1924. TS. History of Education and Teacher Training Collection, Monroe C. Gutman Lib., Harvard U, Cambridge.

—. *Annual Report of the Department of Education For the Year Ending November 30, 1925*. Boston: The Commonwealth of MA, 1926. TS. History of Education and Teacher Training Collection, Monroe C. Gutman Lib., Harvard U, Cambridge.

—. *Annual Report of the Department of Education For the Year Ending November 30, 1927*. Boston: Commonwealth of MA, 1928. TS. History of Education and Teacher Training Collection, Monroe C. Gutman Lib., Harvard U, Cambridge.

—. *Report of the Special Commission on Teachers' Salaries*. Boston: The Commonwealth of MA, 1920. Print.

—. Division of University Extension. *Americanization Courses Given in Co-operation with the State Normal School at Hyannis, Massachusetts, during the Summer Sessions August 2 to September 1, 1920*. Boston: The Commonwealth of MA, 1920. TS. History of Education and Teacher Training Collection, Monroe C. Gutman Lib., Harvard U, Cambridge.

Matsuda, Paul Kei. "Historical Inquiry in Second Language Writing." *Second Language Writing Research: Perspectives on the Process of Knowledge Construction*. Ed. Paul Kei Matsuda and Tony Silva. New York: Taylor & Francis, 2009. 33–48. Print.

—. "Second Language Writing in the Twentieth Century: A Situated Historical Perspective." *Exploring the Dynamics of Second Language Writing*. Ed. Barbara Kroll. New York: Cambridge UP, 2003. 15–34. Print.

Mirel, Jeffrey. *Patriotic Pluralism: Americanization Education and European Immigrants*. Cambridge: Harvard UP, 2010. Print.

Musumeci, Diane. *Breaking Tradition: An Exploration of the Historical Relationship Between Theory and Practice in Second Language Teaching*. New York: McGraw-Hill, 1997. Print.

New York. U of the State of NY. *Immigrant education and Americanization: Summer courses for teacher training in the state of New York*. New York: U of the State of NY, 1920. TS. History of Education and Teacher Training Collection, Monroe C. Gutman Lib., Harvard U, Cambridge.

Raimes, Ann. "Out of the Woods: Emerging Traditions in the Teaching of Writing." *TESOL Quarterly* 25.3 (1991): 407–30. Print.

Richards, Jack C., and Theodore S. Rodgers. *Approaches and Methods in Language Teaching*. 2nd edition. Cambridge: Cambridge UP, 2001. Kindle file.

Roberts, Peter. *English for Coming Americans: Teachers' Manual*. New York: Young Men's Christian Assn. P, 1909. Print.

—. *English for Foreigners*. Urbana: U of Illinois P, 1914. Print.

—. *The Problem of Americanization*. New York: Macmillan, 1920. Print.

Roen, Duane, Maureen Daly Goggin, and Jennifer Clary-Lemon. "Teaching of Writing and Writing Teachers through the Ages." *Handbook of Writing Research*. Ed. Charles Bazerman. Mahwah: Lawrence Erlbaum, 2007. 343–64. Print.

Silva, Tony. "Second Language Composition Instruction: Developments, Issues, and Directions in ESL." *Second Language Writing: Research Insights for the Classroom*. Ed. Barbara Kroll. New York: Cambridge UP, 1990. 11–23. Print.

Towne, Charles. *Report by Mr. Towne of his Trip to Chicago [and other cities]*. Boston: Commonwealth of MA, 1919. TS. History of Education and Teacher Training Collection, Monroe C. Gutman Lib., Harvard U, Cambridge.

Trimbur, John. "Linguistic Memory and the Politics of U.S. English." *College English* 68.6 (2006): 575–88. Print.

United States. Senate. Committee on Education and Labor. *Americanization Bill: Hearing Before The Committee on Education and Labor*. 66th Cong., 1st Sess., S. 17. Washington: GPO, 1919. Print.

—. Department of Interior. Division of Educational Extension. *Americanization Work in New York State*. Washington: GPO, 1919. TS. History of Education and Teacher Training Collection, Monroe C. Gutman Library, Harvard U, Cambridge.

—. Bureau of Education. *Americanization in Pittsburgh*. Washington: GPO, 1919. TS.

History of Education and Teacher Training Collection, Monroe C. Gutman Lib., Harvard U, Cambridge.

Wible, Scott. "Composing Alternatives to a National Security Language Policy." *College English* 71.5 (2009): 460–85. Print.

The Mediation of Literacy Education and Correspondence Composition Courses at UNC–Chapel Hill, 1912–1924[1]

Courtney Adams Wooten

Tracing the correspondence composition courses taught at the University of North Carolina–Chapel Hill from 1912 to 1924, this essay argues that examining distance education in the nineteenth and twentieth centuries can reveal possible problems or solutions to issues composition instructors face in twenty-first-century debates about moving first-year composition courses online, particularly in rapidly developing Massive Open Online Courses (MOOCs). This essay develops a theory of literacy mediation built on Deborah Brandt's notion of literacy sponsorship, claiming that more attention needs to be paid to how literacies are mediated by institutions, particularly when institutions support composition instruction that occurs off-campus as in distance education. Writing programs need to ensure that face-to-face and online students receive comparable instruction and that all students, regardless of the spaces in which they take composition courses, understand the institutional and programmatic values of composition on their physical or virtual campuses.

Correspondence study has often been overlooked as a precursor to online distance education and as an important presence in rhetoric and composition histories. Although some scholars, such as Marthann Schulte, acknowledge the historical beginnings of distance education, they often claim, as Schulte does, that distance education did not truly emerge until the late twentieth and early twenty-first centuries with the advent of online forms of education. Others, such as Chi-Sing Li and Beverly Irby, also overlook correspondence courses as historical precursors to online distance education, largely because such education did not occur through electronic and telecommunicative technologies. In "Designing Efficiencies," Kevin Eric DePew, T. A. Fishman, Julia E. Romberger, and Bridget Fahey Ruetenik argue, "It is crucial that instructors of DE writing courses familiarize themselves with the many histories of this subdiscipline and that they consider how the embedded ideologies influence the narratives that are constructed to rationalize the use of DE in university settings" (64). This article answers their call, offering composition scholars one example of composition taught through correspondence from the early twentieth century. By examining the ways one particular institution offered composition courses via a correspondence program,

I clarify what this historical analysis offers current discussions about online composition instruction and what is at stake when institutions mediate literacy learning off-campus.

Distance education is often traced to the nineteenth century, with the vocational Pitman Shorthand training program via correspondence that began in 1852, and the college-level correspondence courses at Illinois Wesleyan University in 1874 and the University of Chicago in 1892 (Kett 182; Pittman, "Academic" 110; Watkins 3). Most universities did not fully welcome such extension programs until the early twentieth century, when growing numbers of programs emerged at major universities in nineteen states by 1915 (Pittman, "Academic" 111). The mid-1920s were the heyday of correspondence courses with estimated enrollments at 0.5 million students (Hampel 5), quite a large number when compared to the 917,462 total American undergraduate students in 1925–1926 (Hampel 5). Correspondence courses were offered by both postsecondary institutions and private companies, with the International Correspondence Schools dominating 20% of all annual correspondence enrollments throughout the first third of the twentieth century (Hampel 5). The popularity of these courses can be seen in correspondence enrollment numbers; for example, the University of Wisconsin Correspondence Study Department alone registered 24,555 students between 1906 and 1916 (Watkins 16). Widespread enrollment in extension courses, including correspondence courses, culminated in the creation of the National University Extension Association (NUEA) in 1915. This association's members included Louis Round Wilson, the first director of the Bureau of Extension at the University of North Carolina at Chapel Hill (formerly known simply as the University of North Carolina before the consolidation of North Carolina universities in 1931), and the NUEA was hosted by UNC–Chapel Hill in 1927. The first public institution to admit students in the United States, one with a historical presence that has yet to be explored in composition scholarship, UNC–CH's involvement with the NUEA delineates their commitment to distance education broadly conceived. Despite the popularity of correspondence instruction, its dividends were short-lived. With the Great Depression of the 1930s, enrollment in correspondence instruction fell and half the for-profit schools closed; only 18% of the 275 schools open in 1922 were still operating in 1942 (Hampel 7). Distance education did not revive as strongly again until the 1960s.

A more recent manifestation of distance education is, of course, online education. The latest report from the U.S. Department of Education reveals that from 2007–2008, 4,277,000 students—or 20% of all undergraduates in postsecondary institutions—enrolled in at least one distance education class. This figure excludes correspondence courses, primarily including courses delivered through electronic and telecommunicative technologies such as webcasts,

CD-ROMs or DVDs, and computer-based systems (2). It also excludes the rising trend of MOOCs. Online courses and MOOCs are not often connected to correspondence courses, except in passing. Yet varieties of distance education courses often spring from similar motivations and have similar outcomes, despite differences in delivery. Narrowly defining what "counts" as distance education by focusing on online technologies means we miss the crucial connections between today's online distance education and the correspondence courses first offered over one hundred years ago.

Turning attention to one university extension program's use of correspondence to teach composition in the 1910s and 1920s, as I do in this article, illustrates how distance education "mediates" literacy learning—a term I employ to build upon Deborah Brandt's concept of the literacy "sponsor." Considering the idea of mediation complicates how far institutionalized composition instruction can extend outside of the university, which has historically been limited only by the extension program's reach. The concept of mediation, or the movement of literacies between literacy sponsors and those they sponsor, illustrates how literacy sponsorship may be even more vexed than Brandt indicates as we examine spaces in which institutionalized literacies are transmitted through sponsors to those physically *outside* of these institutions. This is particularly true given the low completion rates of online courses, especially MOOCs, and issues with online courses, such as uneven interactions between professors and students, that impact how well students learn literacies valued by specific institutions. Such concerns have been around for a long time; turning to the past illuminates some of the problems that composition scholars, and WPAs in particular, encounter today in the midst of pressures to move composition online.

In this article, I first discuss how scholars have already drawn attention to literacy education occurring outside of schools, offering "mediation" as a valuable way to theorize the degree to which literacies are facilitated at a distance. Next, I contextualize distance learning by focusing on one program, UNC–CH's extension program, initiated in 1912, and the ways the university envisioned this program operating within the community. I then survey literacy education in particular as it developed between 1917 and 1924, focusing on catalogue descriptions of composition courses and how these evolved in light of UNC–CH's approach to distance education and its relationship with on-the-ground composition courses.[2] Ultimately, I contend that this historical examination helps us to build upon Brandt's conception of literacy "sponsors" and new media scholars' theorization of "mediation" to consider what happens when composition courses move from *inside* to *outside* university walls, particularly in online courses today.

Mediation of Literacy Education

Some scholars have explored how literacy learning occurs in the boundaries between home and school spaces. For example, Katherine Adams' *A Group of Their Own: College Writing Courses and American Women Writers, 1880–1940* traces the literacy education of women writers both during and after college. As women enrolled in colleges, English was a popular choice for a major because it provided them with the opportunity "to envision themselves as influential writers as well as the tools with which to achieve this vision" (Adams 40). As women developed as writers, they formed groups of colleagues both in and out of school, "creating new types of personal/professional groups" and crafting "very influential texts that helped shape their era" (xviii–xix). The women Adams studies took institutionalized writing instruction and used it to transform themselves and their society. Focusing more specifically on what happens when students appropriate and amend school literacies, Kelly Ritter's *Who Owns School? Authority, Students, and Online Discourse* examines "the acquisition of literacy as it occurs without or, perhaps more accurately, despite the direct oversight of teachers or teacher-figures" (6). She claims that college students "do not feel in control of their own education" and, consequently, use online discourse to "resist and reject teacher oversight . . . particularly in the highly interpretive and value-laden reading- and writing-centered classroom" (15). Like the women Adams studies, Ritter's study shows how literacies operate between home and school spaces. Unlike these women, however, the students Ritter studies use home and school literacies to assert control over their own education rather than using it to assert their value in society. I here extend Adams and Ritter's studies to examine how schools facilitate literacy education in largely unexamined *overlapping* home and school spaces.

Deborah Brandt's well-known term "sponsor" is useful in my examination of literacies. Explicated most thoroughly in her book *Literacy in American Lives*, the term "sponsor" refers to "any agents, local or distant, concrete or abstract, who enable, support, teach, and model, as well as recruit, regulate, suppress, or withhold, literacy—and gain advantage by it in some way" (19). While I find Brandt's term instrumental in my research, particularly as it accounts for both institutional (school) and extra-institutional (home and work) literacy learning, I find it less helpful when applying this idea to dispersed sponsors as in distance education. When students learn literacies directly sponsored by institutions (such as through the composition courses offered by UNC–CH) but off-campus through distance education (such as in its correspondence courses), sponsorship cannot be traced directly. Students are given instruction in the writing that the institution values, but learning in their home environments shifts their relationship to this writing in ways that institutions can less reliably predict than with face-to-face students.

New media scholars offer theories of "mediation" that meaningfully interact with Brandt's theorization of literacy sponsors to focus attention on the act of sponsorship itself. Leah A. Lievrouw claims that the term "mediation" began to appear in the 1970s as "a way to articulate media and interpersonal communication within a total social or cultural context" (309). Her focus on mediation as communication in context echoes Brandt and other New Literacy Scholars' emphasis on the theorization of literacies in the midst of unique social contexts. Combining these perspectives on mediation and sponsorship refocuses attention on the ways that media and persons communicate; in correspondence courses, this occurs primarily through print documents such as the publications of the extension program at UNC–CH. A central term within mediation theories is "interactivity," or, as Lievrouw explains it, "the extent to which media and information technologies foster a sense of reciprocity, mutuality, affiliation or feedback among system users, or between users and the system itself" (311). Mediation differs in correspondence and online instruction, particularly because interactivity in these two forms changes. As Jeff Rice argues, online spaces allow for the network building that print technologies did not ("Networks and New Media" 128). In other words, more interactivity exists in online instruction than in correspondence instruction because online instruction can provide more immediate interactions through technologies such as wikis, discussion boards, and video conferencing. In correspondence instruction, mediated primarily through print and the postal service, such immediacy is not possible. Despite this difference, other features of correspondence and online instruction are very similar, allowing for valuable comparisons between these types of writing instruction.

UNC–Chapel Hill's Correspondence Composition Courses, 1912–1924

Online instruction involves some aspects of correspondence instruction such as the mediation of literacies between postsecondary institutions and individuals located outside these institutions. Additionally, both correspondence and online instruction have been offered in response to similar institutional needs: lack of space for students and classes on campus, potential students who can't relocate, and budget cuts that affect the support systems needed to offer courses on campus. MOOCs, for example, attempt to reach a much wider range of people, not just college students, with knowledge traditionally exclusive to postsecondary institutions, just as extension programs sought to relocate school knowledge off-campus. Therefore, historical conceptions of correspondence instruction offer a unique lens through which to examine online instruction. To this end, I focus on the ways UNC–CH mediated the literacies of its correspondence students.³ One possible objection to this study is that I assume the traditional classroom *should be* replicated in other environments (i.e., via correspondence and online). This is not my intention. But writing courses that allege to be the same in content, structure, and institutional value should be equivalent even if we debate what "equivalent" means; if face-to-face and online courses are not equivalent, we cannot claim that distance education courses and face-to-face courses serve similar purposes and carry a similar value for students.

UNC–CH is the flagship university of North Carolina's higher education system, founded in 1789 when state legislature passed an act chartering the university. As the first public American institution to admit students, and one with strong ties to early American extension programs, UNC–CH is a useful example of the ways in which distance literacy education was originally conceived and delivered. UNC–CH first intended to use its correspondence program to provide courses primarily to residential students who needed alternative means of completing degrees, a concern echoed regularly in online education today. But the extension program also mediated the education and values of North Carolina citizens, particularly to convey wartime civics and patriotism during World War I, a form of education later evident during World War II (see Miller; Ritter, *To Know Her Own History*). As the program grew, it became an important way for North Carolinians to participate in postsecondary education without having to move to UNC–CH's campus as well as a means for UNC–CH students to earn college credit.

Composition, and first-year composition particularly, has a long history at UNC–CH. The Freshman English requirement (at that time a two-semester sequence also known as English 1–2) for *all* students has been in place since at least January 1902, when these requirements were recorded in the minutes of an academic faculty meeting.⁴ The relationship between the extension program's approach to composition, including correspondence instruction, and approaches to composition on-campus illustrates tensions between competing forms of literacy mediation. Instruction was similar but not equivalent. Correspondence courses were offered from the beginning of the extension program, but, tellingly, only advertised in the *Record,* UNC–CH's student catalogue. Until American involvement in World War I began in 1917, the Bureau of Extension's main community outreach focused on public lectures and a high school debating union while extension courses such as Freshman English served primarily on-campus students.

Norman Foerster, a UNC-CH English professor whose important role in literary studies and creative writing while at the University of Iowa has been documented elsewhere (see Crowley and Brereton), played a role at UNC–CH as the early (unnamed) WPA, or "Chairman," of composition (*UNC Record*

1916–1917 60). A letter he wrote on August 27, 1917, to Edwin Greenlaw, the influential English department chair from 1914 to 1925, discusses the relationship between correspondence courses and residential students: "In case the total number of freshmen is as large as last year, you might consider the possibility of adding a twelfth section [of Freshman English] in place of a dropped elective. . . . If it seems desirable, as you predict, to substitute some extension work for some of the regular work, I for my part shall be glad to handle all or part of it" (Foerster). The first-year composition requirement and corresponding demand for the course, as noted in Foerster's letter, made it a natural choice for conversion to a correspondence course, particularly since UNC–CH had already begun allowing students to count correspondence courses from other institutions for credit.[5] The movement to provide this course and others via correspondence to UNC–CH students was the next likely step, particularly since doing so would allow the university to receive income for these credits and ensure the mediation of literacies sanctioned by UNC–CH. In other words, UNC–CH could be more certain that its students learned writing skills it deemed appropriate if students took the course in their English department, even if via correspondence. Freshman English thus became one of the first twelve correspondence courses offered to UNC–CH students (Culp and Dawson 5).

At the same time, World War I influenced what was taught both on campus and off. In 1917–1918, several extension *Leaflets* offered information about literature courses for citizens. "War Information Series No. 14" offers a course about "National Ideals in British and American Literature," including "an outline of British and American national ideals as expressed in literature . . . for the use of college classes, reading clubs, and private students" (v).[6] Similarly, even Freshman English offered on UNC–CH's campus turned students' attention to wartime issues: the *UNC Record* for 1917–1918 claims that in this course, a literature-based writing course with a focus on civic themes, students will engage in "'intensive-reading' in *American Ideals* and other texts" (61). These corresponding shifts illustrate how UNC–CH mediated literacy education on and off campus to reflect and pass on American qualities during war, even though the ways it did so varied according to the goals UNC–CH set for those taking these courses. North Carolinians were instructed to read about war-related issues on their own or in groups because they were not applying these courses to degrees, whereas UNC–CH students were expected to complete this work as part of a college writing course that met institutional requirements for degree completion.

UNC–CH increasingly moved literacy education out of the institution and into the community throughout the period of American involvement in World War I. Such moves may have been partially motivated by the exodus of UNC–CH students into the armed forces, as evidenced by several notes in faculty meeting minutes devoted to making concessions for students who were joining the war (including granting them credit for courses not completed due to deployment). Though the student population was augmented by the small number of local women students allowed to attend the school from 1917 to 1925 to help fill classes,[7] the overall loss of students led to the growth of the extension program as indicated by University President Edward Kidder Graham. Throughout his time as acting president in 1913 and as president from 1914 to 1918—his time at UNC–CH cut short by his death in an influenza epidemic (Coates 25)—Graham was known for his dedication to extension work. Sensing an opportunity during World War I to expand the extension program, Graham explained to the faculty on October 24, 1917, that the Committee on University Extension "hoped to assist the country at the present crisis, along lines belonging distinctively to the University" (Minutes 1:8, 485), including lectures and correspondence courses. The English courses offered in UNC–CH's *Leaflets* reflect wartime issues, a civic and patriotic mission, rather than mirroring UNC–CH's "standard" English courses, part of an institutional mission.

The Bureau of Extension at UNC–CH grew rapidly after the war. Chester D. Snell, a former graduate of Columbia University, took over the Bureau in 1921, changing its name to the University Extension Division and beginning the publication of the *Extension Bulletin,* which replaced the extension section in the *Record* (Wilson 418). The growth of UNC–CH and its extension program was amplified by a budget crisis during the 1920–1921 school year. In addition to men returning from World War I and seeking entrance into UNC–CH, which continued to admit local women until 1925,[8] Wilson cited the tumbling prices of cotton and tobacco in 1920, vital crops to the North Carolinian economy, as a significant reason that many tried to "enter college in an effort to fit themselves for positions" (320) that they could not otherwise attain. On October 2, 1920, President Graham reported that 2,308 North Carolina high school graduates had been turned away from the university because there was no room for them on campus (Wilson 322). UNC–CH, in addition to lobbying the state for more financial support, responded to these problems in much the same way we have today: by turning to distance education as one way to accommodate more students without greatly expanding faculty, staff, or campus space (see Peterson).

In 1921–1922, information about correspondence courses began to be published in extension *Bulletins* available to community members, marketed as a way to gain a university-sanctioned education outside of the institution itself: "A University Extension Division is the organization which modern state universities have developed to serve as the channel through which some of the university culture and instruction flows to the people" (3). Rather than simply listing the courses offered as the *Leaflets* did, the *Bulletins* offer more specific outlines of what these courses provide, how much they cost, and how many assignments have to be completed for each course, as seen in this description for Freshman English from 1921:

> Freshman English. Intensive reading, chiefly in American prose; extensive reading among selected books and periodicals; constant written composition on topics related to the reading. This course parallels English I in the general catalog. *One course.* Associate Professor Dargan and an assistant. Fee, $10.00. (*Bulletin* 1.3 7)

In making these changes, UNC–CH institutionalized a form of education that had previously served, at least on its face, community purposes. Now, the extension program allowed individuals not physically attending UNC–CH to participate in institutionally authorized writing courses and to potentially use these as credits toward a UNC–CH degree. This was one way UNC–CH could reach the North Carolinians they were unable to enroll as students in 1920.[9]

Even as UNC–CH made moves to extend institutionalized writing instruction into the community, its confidence in the equivalency of these courses with on-campus writing courses was tenuous. One place anxiety about equivalency can be observed is in the course descriptions for English 1 or Freshman English. By 1921, this course had been offered for eight years via correspondence (albeit primarily to UNC–CH students) and for over twenty years on campus with the correspondence courses now advertised to community members through the *Bulletins* and to UNC–CH students through the *Catalogue*. Tensions arose between the course descriptions for the face-to-face course and the correspondence course. In 1923, English I, or Freshman English, at UNC–CH (now a one-semester course) is described as involving, "Intensive reading, chiefly in prose; extensive reading among selected books in the Library; training in reading through a progressive series of exercises; training in writing through exercises in sentence-revision and through frequent written compositions. Fortnightly conferences" (*UNC Catalogue 1923–24* 136). It includes an addendum that this course was not required for students from the School of Engineering (for whom English 9abc, a specialized writing course, was offered). Alternatively, in the *Bulletin* the course is listed as "Freshman English. Intensive reading, chiefly in American prose; extensive reading among selected books and periodicals; constant written composition on topics related to the reading. This course parallels English I in the general catalog" (*Bulletin* 3.1 18).

A couple differences illustrate fundamental tensions at UNC–CH between face-to-face and distance education composition courses. The first is that these courses, while similar, were not exactly the same given the constraints of correspondence education; therefore, the "fortnightly conferences" were completely omitted from the correspondence course, a difference that shaped how teachers and students interacted and the purpose and value of the course. The second is that the correspondence description failed to mention that School of Engineering students should take a different course (or that any other first-year English courses exist, as English 1a also did for basic writers). Although distance education students could take composition courses for credit, they were not given as many options as residential students and were expected to take the writing courses UNC–CH made available to them. These differences illustrate the tensions in what DePew et al. frame as disconnects between efficiency and instructional soundness. UNC–CH wanted to offer its composition courses to those who were unable to attend its university, particularly because of its inability to house all potential students and because of economic pressures—demands very similar to those placed on universities today. As can be seen, however, composition courses offered face-to-face and via correspondence differed in that students taking correspondence courses were not given the same options as on-campus students. When an institution such as UNC–CH grants the same credit for face-to-face and distance education courses, differences in these courses contradict claims to equivalency and impact student learning.

Just as online courses and MOOCs promise to deliver education to many people, correspondence courses proclaimed a broad public service. Kett claims, "many extension officials latched onto the alternative goal of public service" (300) as they recognized the failed narrative of individual advancement. Despite the "high-sounding language" they used to construct their goals, they "were well aware that public-service activities also spruced up the university's image and that citizens who felt that the university took an interest in the public welfare were likely to support legislative appropriations for laboratories, libraries, and faculty salaries" (Kett 300). These trends can be seen at UNC–CH. In "War Information Series No. 2," Greenlaw formally outlines the civic purposes of the extension program:

> The center of the organization, as of so much community life, is the public school. American government is based on the conception of an educated citizenry . . . of late we have tried to see more clearly the relations of the school to life. The emphasis, often exaggerated, on vocational training, is one result; the increasing use of the school as a *community center* is another. (vi, emphasis added)

Greenlaw attributes American democracy to education, but, interestingly, he insists that "school" must become "a community center" that continually opens up education to everyone rather than a traditional model in which education is only offered to students within the school's walls. Thus, he outlines one of the benefits of distance education: many more people are able to engage with knowledge offered by a particular institution.

UNC–CH continued to seek ways to mediate the literacy education of North Carolinians both on and off its campus through the mid-1920s and beyond. Its enrollment boomed in 1924–1925 with 2,823 distance education students outnumbering residential students by 300 (Wilson 419).[10] The first page of the 1923–1924 *Bulletin* contains an "Are You Included?" section that outlines the diverse individuals the extension program can reach: "University courses of standard grade by correspondence offer excellent opportunities to hundreds of persons who are fully qualified to pursue them profitably but who, for various reasons, are unable to attend a university" (*Extension Bulletin* 3.1 28). As the program grew, UNC–CH promoted its ability to mediate the schooling of many individuals throughout North Carolina who would otherwise be unable to attend the university, even as its residential students continued to take correspondence courses to supplement their face-to-face courses. Literacy education through extension thus became an extra-institutional site of literacy practices. As more brick-and-mortar universities consider offering online courses, particularly MOOCs, they face the concerns UNC–CH illustrates of providing an education to students who are unable or unwilling to physically relocate. Those universities such as San Jose State University, which offer MOOCs, are often characterized as "pioneers" who are at the forefront of educational progress, leaving other schools in the dust, much as correspondence programs were used to enhance the image of brick-and-mortar schools (see Jaschik; Lewin; Pappano). Nevertheless, as indicated by the low pass rates of SJSU students in its initial MOOCs,[11] problems with MOOCs need to be resolved before more institutions embrace them as pedagogically sound alternatives to face-to-face courses.

My examination of UNC–CH's correspondence composition courses illustrates some of the issues we face today with online instruction. Institutions and writing programs need to consider what is lost and what is gained in transitions from face-to-face to online courses. Although more potential students can be reached through distance education courses, the sponsorship of literacies necessarily shifts when taught remotely. UNC–CH's correspondence composition courses illustrate the need for composition scholars and teachers to consider how literacies are similarly and dissimilarly mediated on- and off-campus. Doing so can reveal how well online writing courses meet institutional and programmatic goals for first-year writing students and how well students are served by online writing courses.

Composition Instruction in Mediated Online Spaces

UNC–CH acknowledges some limitations to its correspondence program in a 1923 *Bulletin*: "It is not practicable to offer through extension some courses now being given at the University. Certain courses, by their very nature, cannot be offered as extension classes. Courses that require laboratory facilities are an example" (3.8 7). Although composition was clearly viewed as a subject that could be mediated without face-to-face interaction at UNC–CH in the early twentieth century, it was part of a degree program that could not be completely mediated off-campus. This tension calls into question the degree to which *any* aspect of education, including writing courses, can be mediated off-campus and still maintain the original goals of an educational institution, department, or instructor (see Hewett and Ehmann; Warnock). It also highlights the ways that literacy education in and out of schools overlap, shaping each other even when directed by an institution for specific goals. Historical studies of composition mediated outside classrooms, but sponsored by institutions, are critical in understanding the directions being taken now in distance education as well as the implications for these kinds of literacy mediations.

Correlations between correspondence courses and online courses can be seen through completion rates for correspondence courses compared to that of MOOCs and online courses. Hampel notes that correspondence course completion was low, with the International Correspondence Schools recording a 5% completion rate during the 1930s (15). Such atrocious completion rates are remarkably similar to the low completion rates in MOOCs; Denise Comer reports only 1.5% of students completed the English Composition I MOOC she taught at Duke University in 2013. Sapp and Simon also found that in four sections of first-year composition (two online and two face-to-face), only 56% of online students completed the course compared to 100% of the face-to-face students (473). Low completion rates for online courses, as with correspondence courses, indicate students' lack of attention in these courses, which occur in media-rich online spaces but fail to fully utilize these resources (see Rice, "What I Learned in MOOC"), as well as insufficient support for them, particularly for students with different learning styles (see Xu and Jaggars).

The correlation between correspondence courses and online courses can also be seen through their lack of interactivity, especially in MOOCs. Despite the many ways that online courses can accommodate personal interaction that correspondence study could not, such as synchronous chats and video, students still experience problems with interactivity in online courses. In Shanna Smith Jaggars' study of forty-six community college students who were taking at least one online course, almost all students noted that in online courses "they missed the direct instruction that they received in face-to-face courses, and many alluded to the notion that without that component, they felt as though they were 'teaching themselves'" (10). Other studies have found similar outcomes about students needing more interactivity in online composition courses, particularly to compensate for the lack of face-to-face interaction (see Boyd; Sapp and Simon). Teaching oneself is exactly what students taking correspondence courses were expected to do, as can be seen in the details of the composition course descriptions at UNC–CH. Some online courses undoubtedly are better at mitigating this problem than others, but composition teachers moving their courses online should carefully consider to what extent they can be "present" and how this impacts what their students learn, particularly given the different approaches to writing that various institutions and writing programs use.

Scott Warnock takes an optimistic view that online writing courses help "students write and think in ways previously unimagined" (xxvi), and that they are a "migration" of face-to-face courses into a different environment rather than completely different courses. I argue that institutions must more fully account for changes that occur when composition instruction is moved online, especially into MOOCs. Such courses are clearly not identical because of differences in instruction and interaction when moved online: for instance, the mediation of literacies is not as direct and personal, even with the use of synchronous technologies. Furthermore, the sheer number of students in many of these writing courses ensures that they have to operate differently by incorporating less writing and offering less feedback and assessment from the instructor. UNC–CH moved its composition courses outside its walls but did not fully integrate correspondence students into its campus community—signaled by its failure to inform correspondence students of all composition course options available to on-campus students. Similarly, institutions cannot claim that online writing courses, particularly for students who never attend courses on campus, reinforce institutional or programmatic values to students who do not understand the institutional context in which they take these courses. In order for institutions to adequately mediate the literacy sponsorship of their online students, more work needs to be done to inform them about the mission and role of first-year writing, both on- and off-campus. In these spaces, first-year writing should accomplish similar objectives, even if mediated in different ways, and all students should be cognizant of the valuing of writing and literacy in general within an institution.

DePew et al. claim that "without attention to the tensions that exist between what is most efficient and what is most instructionally robust, decisions will continue to be made that do not reflect what we, within the field of composition, believe to be in the best interests of our students" (64). These tensions were clearly at work at UNC–CH, where what was efficient for correspondence courses often took precedence over what was instructionally sound or equivalent to face-to-face courses (such as the omission of conferencing from correspondence composition courses). Stakeholders such as administrators and students need to understand what aspects of online composition courses are dissimilar from face-to-face courses through the employment of different course titles and numbers for face-to-face and online courses, explicit information about these differences within individual programs, and our discussion of these differences not just in academic venues but in more open public forums. Students should also be aware of possible constraints, such as different levels of interactivity between instructors and students, on their success in these courses. Composition programs and courses need to make these potential difficulties explicit to students, providing adequate advising about which students are best prepared to take these and which are not.

Finally, UNC–CH's correspondence courses in the early twentieth century may have attracted more students to the university and ushered them into composition courses they would have otherwise not taken, but these courses failed to inculcate students into UNC–CH's unique institutional and educational context. Students who took writing via correspondence did not have face-to-face contact with English professors or fellow students. Instead, they completed these courses at home outside of a focused learning community engaged in similar pursuits. Without further integration into UNC–CH, students would not as easily understand the value that the institution placed on writing or its particular kind of valuing (or its brand). Online composition courses operate in a similar context. Institutions and composition programs need to consider the extent to which they can claim the equivalency of online and face-to-face courses when the literacies they mediate off-campus are not entirely their own. Leading orientation sessions about first-year writing or providing students in first-year writing courses with information about first-year writing goals, objectives, and positioning in the institution (which typically occur already but need to be emphasized, particularly in online writing courses) can help all students better understand what writing at specific institutions entails. Examining this history of UNC–CH correspondence writing courses helps us to better understand how institutions mediate literacy learning that occurs off-campus and how we can use this knowledge to improve both face-to-face and online composition courses as well as the literacy learning of all students.

Notes

1. Many thanks to two anonymous *Composition Studies* reviewers, Jennifer Clary-Lemon, Laura Micciche, and Kelly Ritter for their invaluable feedback on previous drafts of this essay.

2. Following Donahue and Moon in *Local Histories* and Ramsey, Sharer, L'Eplattenier, and Mastrangelo in *Working in the Archives,* I outline my research

methodology for readers who may be interested in similar archival research. Because I am focused on how the university situates itself as a sponsor of literacy education to UNC–CH students and North Carolinians rather than how successful their mediation was (which would be a different, but equally valuable, project), I examined the published *Leaflets* and *Bulletins* of UNC–CH's extension program as well as information about its on-the-ground composition program. The *Leaflets* and *Bulletins* can be found not only at UNC–CH but also at UNCG (its sister school only fifty miles away), making these materials rare but not archival. Other materials, such as UNC *Catalogues*, faculty meeting notes, and letters, are either archival or rare, located at the Louis Round Wilson Special Collections Library and the North Carolina Collection in the Wilson Library at UNC–CH. One of the problems with further scholarship about correspondence and other forms of distance education, particularly composition courses offered via these media, is the scarcity of archival materials that Pittman notes ("Correspondence Study" 32).

3. As mentioned in the previous note, I do so by examining both rare and archival materials from this time period. Unfortunately, further historical information about composition at UNC–CH during this time period, either on the ground or via correspondence, is unavailable. However, these documents provide enough information about correspondence composition courses to trace how the university mediated literacy to correspondence students, even though further details about what was taught or how well students learned to write in these spaces are unavailable.

4. There was a longer tradition of English composition and rhetoric at UNC–CH beginning in 1796 with the appointment of W.L. Richards as "Teacher of French and English" (MacMillan 4) and continuing with a new program of studies devised in 1875 when UNC–CH reopened after the Civil War to include "grammar, composition, elementary rhetoric, elocution, and 'English Literature, Essays and Original Addresses'" in the completion of bachelor degrees (MacMillan 9).

5. This occurred around 1913 as indicated by a request granted by the faculty on February 18, 1913 from student G.E. Blackshock petitioning for correspondence credit from the University of Chicago.

6. I would extend James A. Berlin's argument that the Great War pulled English studies into "the center of public school education in the United States" (56) to UNC–CH's literacy education, which increasingly focused on American values as conveyed through literature.

7. According to the Carolina Women's Center at UNC, "[d]ue to housing shortages and concerns over propriety, the first-year women must prove they are living with family or caretakers." In reality, the university limited the admittance of women students to daughters of local residents, discouraging families from moving for this purpose (Dean).

8. After World War I ended, UNC–CH changed the admittance policy so that only women who were pre-med students could attend. It was only in 1963 that women were allowed to enroll in other programs at UNC–CH (Dean).

9. At this time, degrees could still not be completed entirely outside of the university, highlighting UNC–CH's belief that a degree from its institution could not, and even should not, be completed without some face-to-face mediation of schooling.

10. The general growth of extension programs was noted by Snell at a faculty meeting on February 27, 1923, when he cites regulations at roughly four hundred other universities, colleges, and normal schools who "have anywhere from 300 to 5,000 students in extension classes each year" (110).

11. Pass rates for Spring 2013 MOOCs at San Jose State University ranged from 29–51% for SJSU students to 12–45% for non-enrolled students (Kolowich).

Works Cited

Adams, Katherine H. *A Group of Their Own: College Writing Courses and American Women Writers, 1880–1940.* Albany, NY: SUNY P, 2001. Print.

Berlin, James. *Rhetoric and Reality: Writing Instruction in American Colleges, 1900–1985.* Carbondale: SIUP, 1987. Print.

Boyd, Patricia Webb. "Analyzing Students' Perceptions of Their Learning in Online and Hybrid Composition Courses." *Computers and Composition* 25.2 (2008): 224–43. Print.

Brandt, Deborah. *Literacy in American Lives.* Cambridge: Cambridge UP, 2001. Print.

Brereton, John C. *The Origins of Composition Studies in the American College, 1875–1925: A Documentary History.* Pittsburgh: U of Pittsburgh P, 1996. Print.

Carolina Women's Center. "Breaking Barriers, Making History: Timeline of Women's Education at UNC–Chapel Hill." *The University of North Carolina at Chapel Hill.* The University of North Carolina at Chapel Hill, 2012. Web. 16 June 2012.

Coates, Albert. *Edward Kidder Graham, Harry Woodburn Chase, Frank Power Graham.* Chapel Hill, NC: A. Coates, 1988. Print.

Comer, Denise. "Teaching and Learning Writing in a MOOC: Implications, Outcomes, and Reflections." Queering the Writing Program. CWPA Annual Conference. Georgia Coastal Center, Savannah, GA. 19 July 2013. Conference Presentation.

Crowley, Sharon. *Composition in the University.* Pittsburgh: U of Pittsburgh P, 1998. Print.

Culp, Mary Marshall Rand, and Alvin H. Dawson, Jr. *Continuing Education at the University of North Carolina at Chapel Hill: A Retrospective.* Chapel Hill: U of North Carolina P, 1991. Print.

Dean, Pamela. *Women on the Hill: A History of Women at the University of North Carolina.* Chapel Hill: Division of Student Affairs, U of North Carolina, 1987. PDF File.

DePew, Kevin Eric, T. A. Fishman, Julia E. Romberger, and Bridget Fahey Ruetenik. "Designing Efficiencies: The Parallel Narratives of Distance Education and Composition Studies." *Computers and Composition* 23.1 (2006): 49–67. Print.

Donahue, Patricia, and Gretchen Flesher Moon. *Local Histories: Reading the Archives of Composition.* Pittsburgh: U of Pittsburgh P, 2007. Print.

Foerster, Norman. Letter to Edwin Greenlaw. 27 Aug. 1917. MS. Department of English Records, University Archives, Louis Round Wilson Special Collections Library, University of North Carolina at Chapel Hill. Box 1, Folder 1.

Hampel, Robert L. "The National Home Study Council, 1926–1942." *The American Journal of Distance Education* 23 (2009): 4–19. Print.

Hewett, Beth L., and Christa Ehmann. *Preparing Educators for Online Writing Instruction: Principles and Processes.* Urbana, IL: NCTE, 2004. Print.

Jaggars, Shanna Smith. "Choosing Between Online and Face-to-Face Courses: Community College Student Voices." *Community College Research Center.* Teachers College, Columbia U, Apr. 2013. Web. 12 May 2013.

Jaschik, Scott. "Public Universities Move to Offer MOOCs for Credit." *Inside Higher Ed.* Inside Higher Ed, 23 Jan. 2013. Web. 13 May 2013.

Kett, Joseph F. *The Pursuit of Knowledge Under Difficulties: From Self-Improvement to Adult Education in America, 1750–1990.* Stanford: Stanford UP, 1994. Print.

Kolowich, Steve. "San Jose State U. Puts MOOC Project with Udacity on Hold." *The Chronicle of Higher Education.* Chronicle of Higher Educ., 19 July 2013. Web. 29 July 2013.

Lewin, Tamar. "Colleges Adapt Online Courses to Ease Burden." *The New York Times.* New York Times, 29 Apr. 2013. Web. 13 May 2013.

Li, Chi-Sing, and Beverly Irby. "An Overview of Online Education: Attractiveness, Benefits, Challenges, Concerns and Recommendations." *College Student Journal* 42.2 (2008): 449–58. Print.

Lievrouw, Leah A. "New Media, Mediation, and Communication Study." *Information, Communication & Society* 12.3 (2009): 303–25. Print.

MacMillan, Dougald. *English at Chapel Hill: 1795–1969.* Durham, NC: UNC Chapel Hill, 1970. Print.

Miller, Thomas P. *The Evolution of College English: Literacy Studies from the Puritans to the Postmoderns.* Pittsburgh: U of Pittsburgh P, 2011. Print.

Minutes, Volume 1:8 in the General Faculty and Faculty Council of the University of North Carolina at Chapel Hill Records, 1901–1919, University Archives, Louis Round Wilson Special Collections Library, University of North Carolina at Chapel Hill. Collection number SV–40106, Series 1.

Minutes, Volume 1:9 in the General Faculty and Faculty Council of the University of North Carolina at Chapel Hill Records, 1901–1919, University Archives, Louis Round Wilson Special Collections Library, University of North Carolina at Chapel Hill. Collection number SV–40106, Series 1.

Pappano, Laura. "The Year of the MOOC." *The New York Times.* New York Times, 2 Nov. 2012. Web. 14 May 2013.

Peterson, Patricia Webb. "The Debate about Online Learning: Key Issues for Writing Teachers." *Computers and Composition* 18.4 (2001): 359–70. Print.

Pittman, Von. "Academic Credibility and the 'Image Problem': The Quality Issue in Collegiate Independent Study." *The Foundations of American Distance Education: A Century of Collegiate Correspondence Study.* Ed. Barbara L. Watkins and Stephen J. Wright. Dubuque, IA: Kendall/Hunt, 1991. 109–34. Print.

—. "Correspondence Study in the American University: A Second Historiographic Perspective." *Handbook of Distance Education.* Ed. Michael Grahame Moore and William G. Anderson. Mahwah, NJ: Lawrence Erlbaum, 2003. 21–35. Print.

Ramsey, Alexis E., Wendy B. Sharer, Barbara L'Eplattenier, and Lisa S. Mastrangelo. *Working in the Archives: Practical Research Methods for Rhetoric and Composition.* Carbondale: SIUP, 2010. Print.

Rice, Jeff. "Networks and New Media." *College English* 69.2 (2006): 127–33. Print.

—. "What I Learned in MOOC." *CCC* 64.4 (2013): 695–703. Print.

Ritter, Kelly. *To Know Her Own History: Writing at the Woman's College, 1943–1963.* Pittsburgh: U of Pittsburgh P, 2012. Print.

—. *Who Owns School? Authority, Students, and Online Discourse.* Cresskill, NJ: Hampton P, 2010. Print.

Sapp, David, and James Simon. "Comparing Grades in Online and Face-to-Face Writing Courses: Interpersonal Accountability and Institutional Commitment." *Computers and Composition* 22.4 (2005): 471–89. Print.

Schulte, Marthann. "The Foundations of Technology Distance Education: A Review of the Literature to 2001." *The Journal of Continuing Higher Education* 59.1 (2011): 34–44. Print.

The University of North Carolina: The Catalogue 1919–1924. Chapel Hill: UNC, 1919–1924. Print.

The University of North Carolina Extension Bulletin. Chapel Hill: UNC, 1921–1924. Print.

The University of North Carolina Extension Leaflet. Chapel Hill: UNC, 1917–1919. Print.

The University of North Carolina Record: The Catalogue 1916–1918. Number 145. Chapel Hill: UNC, 1917–1918. Print.

The University of North Carolina Record: Abridged Catalogue: Announcement of Courses for 1919–1920. Chapel Hill: UNC, 1919. Print.

U.S. Department of Education, National Center for Education Statistics. *Learning at a Distance: Undergraduate Enrollment in Distance Education Courses and Degree Programs* (NCES 2012-154). Oct. 2011. Web. 4 June 2012.

Warnock, Scott. *Teaching Writing Online: How and Why.* Urbana, IL: NCTE, 2009. Print.

Watkins, Barbara L. "A Quite Radical Idea: The Invention and Elaboration of Collegiate Correspondence Study." *The Foundations of American Distance Education: A Century of Collegiate Correspondence Study.* Ed. Barbara L. Watkins and Stephen J. Wright. Dubuque, IA: Kendall/Hunt, 1991. 1–35. Print.

Wilson, Louis Round. *The University of North Carolina, 1900–1930: The Making of a Modern University.* Chapel Hill: U of North Carolina P, 1957. Print.

Xu, Di, and Shanna Smith Jaggars. "Adaptability to Online Learning: Differences Across Types of Students and Academic Subject Areas." *Community College Research Center.* Teachers College, Columbia U, Feb. 2013. Web. 12 May 2013.

Course Design

English 341: Advanced Composition for Teachers

William Duffy

Course Description

English 341: Advanced Composition for Teachers is a three-credit undergraduate course for pre-service educators at Francis Marion University, a mid-size public university located in northeast South Carolina. According to the university catalog, students enrolled in English 341 "explore connections among writing, teaching, and learning as they examine the implications that their experiences as writers have for their work as teachers" (95). The English department at FMU offers three concentrations: a Liberal Arts (literature) track, a Professional Writing track, and a Secondary Teacher Certification option. The students who enroll in English 341, however, are almost exclusively early-childhood education, elementary education, and middle level education majors, all of who must complete the course as a degree requirement.

Institutional Context

Founded in 1970, Francis Marion University (named after the Revolutionary War hero, General Francis Marion) is located in Florence, South Carolina, and is one of the state's four-year, state-supported universities. While FMU does have small, localized graduate programs in the Schools of Business and Education, and in the departments of nursing and psychology, the majority of its 4,000 students are undergraduates, and many of these are first-generation college students. The English department is home to FMU's Composition Program, which includes a three-course sequence all FMU students are required to complete: English 111 (Introduction to Composition), English 112 (Argumentative Writing), and English 200 (Writing in the Disciplines), although students can place out of English 111 and English 112 with a score of 500+ on the SAT, transfer credit, or by composing an essay that the department chair and composition coordinator review. Before it was renamed "Advanced Composition for Teachers," English 341 was identified in the course catalog as English 220: Advanced Composition. Students who enrolled in English 220 did earn a writing credit, but otherwise it was something of an ambiguous course insofar as the class was neither required for English majors nor a unique course with a content-specific moniker. As one of my colleagues in the English department remarked, English 220 always had an identity problem largely because it was a course without a defined audience.

Indeed, the course description for English 220 communicates its existence as a catchall writing course with no specified purpose:

ENG 220 Advanced Composition (3)

(Prerequisite: A grade of C or higher in English 200) Extensive work in practical writing, including personal, informative, and analytical composition. The frequent assignments involve training in evaluation of writing and in both primary and secondary research techniques. (*Catalog* 2003–04)

Such a description obviously fails to define what exactly "advanced composition" means, especially when English 220 is compared to the English department's existing composition courses. Its emphasis on "both primary and secondary research techniques," for example, sounds much like the purpose of English 200 (Writing in the Disciplines). Moreover, what is "practical writing"? A euphemism for workplace or professional writing? The English department already offers "advanced" writing courses in creative nonfiction, professional writing, and technical writing, in addition to a "Special Topics in Writing" course that allows instructors to theme an advanced writing course around a specific content area. In short, English 220 existed as an ambiguous course with no distinguishable purpose when considered alongside other offerings in the English department's writing curriculum.

The one exception to its apparent lack of purpose is that the course was required for education majors specializing in early-childhood, elementary, and middle-level teaching. The School of Education believed its majors needed at least one writing-intensive course beyond English 200 (Writing in the Disciplines), and thus English 220 was designated a required course for these students. The problem is that English 220 was not originally conceptualized as a writing course for pre-service educators, which one can obviously discern from its course description above. Moreover, because there was always a small contingent of non-education majors enrolled in the course (usually professional writing majors who needed another writing credit), the course's instructors found themselves in a bind. Do they shape English 220 to the specific needs of pre-service teachers who will be writing and teaching writing as professional educators? If so, doesn't that "leave behind" (forgive the allusion) those students in the course who are not pre-service teachers? On the flip side, if English 220 is a course primarily populated by education majors, why not tailor the course to them? It was this dilemma that motivated the English department to rethink English 220 and its curricular identity.

Under the direction of several professors in the department, including Kenneth Autrey, Matthew Nelson, and Meredith Love, English 220: Advanced

Composition was eventually dropped from the books in the 2010–11 academic year and in its place emerged English 341: Advanced Composition for Teachers. In collaboration with the School of Education, the English department conceptualized English 341 as an advanced writing course designed exclusively for pre-service educators. What distinguishes the course from other writing courses the department offers, aside from its well-defined audience, is its dual purpose. Not only is it an "advanced composition" course that focuses on what it means to write like a teacher, for lack of a better phrase, but it also serves as a pedagogy course that provides students with instruction in the teaching of writing itself. As mentioned above, English 341 is a required course for early childhood, elementary, and middle-level education majors; in fact, these are the only students who now enroll in the course. The English department does offer a composition pedagogy course, English 340 (Theories of Writing), but this course is chiefly designed for majors in the Secondary Teacher Certification track, and thus it covers material that does not directly apply to the writing that English 341's target audiences will teach in their future positions. In fact, English 341 provides education majors not enrolled in a secondary education program with a writing-intensive course centered on the notion that ultimately all teachers, in one way or another, are teachers of writing.

Now in its third year of existence, English 341 is one of the English department's regularly offered advanced writing courses. But because the course is still relatively new, its identity (at least in terms of content) is still fairly undefined. That is, while English 341 is more clearly conceptualized than English 220, the course is nevertheless a novel addition to the department's curriculum and as such none of the three professors who have taught the course have left a distinct set of fingerprints that might give the course a stable identity from one semester to the next. In fact, when Professor Autrey retired in 2011, I joined the English department as a rhetoric and composition specialist who could ostensibly give English 341 a shape and content appropriate for its intended purpose, which, according to the 2011–2012 catalog, is to provide students with opportunities for "careful reading and practice composing in various modes relevant for early-childhood, elementary, and middle-level teachers" (95).

Theoretical Rationale

Scholars in the field of composition studies have a long history of studying the theory/practice binary in the work of teaching writing. In a 1977 *CCC* article, for example, Richard Gebhardt asserts the need for "Balancing Theory with Practice in the Training of Writing Teachers," as the piece's title reads. Gebhardt contends, in short, "that students preparing to teach writing in public school or college should understand important conceptual underpinnings of composition and the teaching of writing and should test them out in practice" (134). Gebhardt's claim is an early argument for the value of praxis, what teachers of writing understand to be the critical space where one's training in theories of composition and its various pedagogies gets evaluated alongside reflection of teaching in action. Next to Gebhardt's piece in that same issue of *CCC* appears Janet Emig's "Writing as a Mode of Learning," in which she uses the educational psychology of Lev Vygotsky, Jerome Bruner, and others to suggest a theoretical framework for recognizing the heuristic value of writing as a "uniquely powerful multi-representational mode for learning" (125). Emig argues, in other words, that writing is not just a medium for spelling out what one has already learned; it is a vehicle for learning itself, an activity that actually fosters the production of knowledge. So while Gebhardt argues about the ideal structure of a composition pedagogy course, Emig focuses on the pedagogical value of composition itself as a tool for enhancing learning processes. For rhetoric and compositionists today, these classic arguments about the pedagogical value of writing and teacher training function as disciplinary commonplaces, ones that hardly need defending.

I reference these pieces because I stumbled upon them when preparing my syllabus for English 341. Specifically, I was researching how compositionists negotiate the presentation of pedagogical theory alongside occasions for practice when the course under consideration is not a traditional practicum. As Sidney Dobrin reminds us, pedagogy courses in our discipline are locations where "theory/practice debates are played out with very material ramifications" (3). He notes in particular how students in these courses learn "skills/trades/pedagogies" that will ostensibly be passed to students of their own (28). It would seem, then, the notion of praxis is an invaluable concept to draw upon in order to mediate composition's theory/practice dichotomy. When Gebhardt and Emig's articles are read side-by-side, these seemingly dated pieces present a timely challenge to instructors of English 341 and similar courses, requiring us to reconsider the meaning of praxis, especially the extent to which the "practice" implicit in the concept of praxis needs a definite shape or outline prior to critical reflection. In other words, do teachers of writing need identifiable "practices" in order to participate in the kinds of critical reflection that sharpens self-awareness and encourages thoughtful teaching?

In the case of English 341, for example, what exactly does it mean to practice "composing in various modes relevant for early-childhood, elementary, and middle-level teachers"? While the course description for English 341 spells out its purpose in terms noticeably more concrete than that of English 220, what was a problem of definition in conceptualizing *the purpose* of the latter course seemingly gives way to a problem of scope in conceptualizing *the content* of the former. Indeed, how does one zero in on appropriate pedagogical instruction relevant to those who, on one end of the spectrum, will be teaching 4- and

5-year-olds, and, on the other end, 12- and 13-year-olds? Surely the training that early-childhood educators need to teach writing is different from what elementary teachers need, which, in turn, should be different from the training that middle school teachers receive.

These differences represent the hurdles I faced when I joined the department two years ago and began teaching English 341. Not only was I unsure "how" to teach composition pedagogy to such a wide range of students, but I also questioned whether it was possible to actually deliver such a course in the first place. In short, English 341 seemed to address too wide a range of future teachers for me—or anyone else, I assumed—to design instruction in composition pedagogy that could adequately speak to each group. To confront these challenges I stepped back to reevaluate how students would be best served in the course, especially given these questions of scope and content. Consequently, I ended up revising the student outcomes for the course using language that highlights writing as a form of inquiry, a variation of Emig's "writing to learn" model. For example, I emphasized that students would "develop strategies for using writing as a method for reflection and discovery in the classroom," an aim that, while open-ended, nudges students to consider the inventive potential of writing as a method for asking questions about what they are learning. Revising the course outcomes in this way allowed me to rethink what kinds of pedagogical theory would be most helpful for students while also taking into consideration what types of writing assignments could successfully bridge the theory-practice split of a composition pedagogy course.

The result is a course that directs pre-service teachers to examine themselves as writers *and* teachers of writing by engaging these identities through inquiry that targets what Paulo Freire calls "untested feasibility." Education requires confrontation with "limit-situations," occasions where our experience is inadequate to overcome particular challenges we perceive within a given task. If we believe there is nothing beyond these limit-situations—that it is impossible to overcome them—fatalism is sure to result. But according to Freire in *Pedagogy of the Oppressed*, we transform limit-situations by engaging the untested feasibility of our "potential consciousness," which is, in short, Freire's method for fostering *conscientização*, or critical consciousness (113, 119). Learning to write certainly represents a limit-situation for students, especially when they conceive of writing as a performance they can either pass or fail. So to teach writing as a form of inquiry, as a place where students get to experiment with composition and take risks, teachers must model what this kind of writing entails. To borrow from Freire, teachers of writing must acknowledge the existence of limit-situations and model how to transform them. In my case, this meant I had to acknowledge my own limit-situations (I've never taught

4-year-olds to write, for example) while creating space and opportunity for students to teach me as I attempt to teach them.

As I articulated this rationale to myself, I noticed the pragmatic dimension of Freire's critical pedagogy, especially in his notion of untested feasibility. The relationship between pragmatism and critical pedagogy is evident for Kate Ronald and Hephzibah Roskelly as well. The original American pragmatists, including but not limited to Charles Peirce, William James, and John Dewey, all believed the most useful philosophies were those that could mediate competing claims while allowing individuals to arrive at contingent truths that facilitate action. This, too, is the goal of Freire's pedagogy. Here is where the two philosophies meet:

> Critical literacy for Freire involves movement between participant/reflector, reflector/participant; for the pragmatists, too, movement between doing/reflecting/doing constitutes the path of learning. Central to both the pragmatic agenda and Freire's praxis is the necessary connection between action and reflection; this connection leads both Freire and the pragmatists to a sense of hopefulness, a belief at least in contingent possibility. For both philosophies, belief means a willingness to act and the assurance that reflection on action will lead to better, more hopeful acts. (Ronald and Roskelly 614)

It is not enough for Freire and the pragmatists to simply point to reflection and argue that it alone makes education viable. Nor is it enough to prescribe specific practices that supposedly constitute the practical application of a particular pedagogy. Instead, the movement between participant/reflector and doing/reflecting/doing that Ronald and Roskelly underscore is actualized when learners discover their own outlets for experimentation. As Freire defines the idea of praxis, it is "reflection and action upon the world *in order to transform it*" (51; emphasis added). New teachers, especially those who will be teaching early, elementary, and middle-level students in public schools, will struggle to balance the demands of curricular oversight and nationalized systems of assessment alongside the hope and change associated with education that get circulated in our cultural narratives about schooling, ideals that prompt many teachers to enter the profession in the first place. By promoting a notion of praxis that is purpose-oriented rather than practice-oriented, we encourage teachers to identify the *why* of their teaching alongside the *what* and *how*. Moreover, purpose-oriented praxis supports the basic arguments about writing as a mode of learning first articulated by Emig, and later echoed by C.H. Knoblauch and Lil Brannon when they assert "knowing is an activity, not a condition or state"; and knowledge itself "implies the making of connections, not an inert body of information" (467).

Pairing this foundational notion that we "write to learn" with the critical-pragmatic method outlined by Ronald and Roskelly, I shaped English 341 as a course in which students use writing as a tool for assessing the consequences of their developing identities as teachers, an approach that allowed me to direct attention to how writing can be adapted to particular classroom types. My approach to English 341 was to present writing as a pedagogical resource available to practically any teacher; as well, I emphasized how to develop critical-pragmatic attitudes toward writing that encourage the development of responsible pedagogies rooted in the "writing to learn" ethic. In the course syllabus I communicated these aims by presenting the goals of the course in two categories, ones that summarized how we would think about ourselves as teachers and writers respectively. Initially, then, I wanted students to approach this course with two distinct (and if not for a time, competing) focuses for the work we would undertake in the class. The first of these points of focus directs attention to the idea of literacy and how we understand and communicate its personal, academic, and public value. Here questions get asked about the work of writing in educational contexts and how to encourage students across grade levels to experiment with its challenges. The second point of focus engages the idea of writing itself and what it looks like to expand our knowledge of how writing works. By interrogating their own writing habits, for example, students are encouraged to recognize how composition is both a productive and an interpretative art that influences and informs how we think about, observe, and act in the world.

By initially separating these two areas of inquiry, I designed the course to challenge students to interrogate their own understanding of teaching alongside the value of writing. In this way I intended students to connect their experiences with writing in the course to the concepts and theories about writing itself conveyed in course readings. The class met on Tuesdays/Thursdays, which I felt created a natural organization for how to balance the teaching-writing dichotomy that I imagined would function as a limit-situation for students, at least initially. Indeed, the course syllabus reflected this split by using Tuesdays for discussion of course readings and Thursdays for "practice" centered on students' own writing. In theory, then, students would get to spend half of the week focused on questions about what it means *to teach writing* while spending the other half working through their development as teachers *who write*.

The books I chose for the course represent the kind of varied discussions of writing I concluded would be most useful for pre-service teachers who will most likely never again take a college-level composition pedagogy course. The first of these texts, *Understanding Writing: Ways of Observing, Learning, and Teaching*, edited by Nancie Atwell and Thomas Newkirk, is a collection of essays written by practicing teachers in early-childhood and elementary contexts. The contributors detail particular assignments and classroom-based pedagogies that incorporate writing. While the text itself is dated (the latest edition was published in 1987), the activities and experiences chronicled in the essays are easily adaptable to today's classrooms. The second book I selected, Peter Elbow's collection of essays *Everyone Can Write*, is the most traditional work of composition theory and pedagogy included on the syllabus. As most *Composition Studies* readers are aware, Elbow's appeal is located in his practical insistence to model theory as he proposes it. For example, in one of his essays, "Freewriting and the Problem of Wheat and Tares," nearly half of the essay is Elbow's own unedited freewriting that he completed to get started on that particular composition. In this way, Elbow offers novice compositionists a personal and low-stakes invitation to experiment with writing in practice. The third book I assigned is Anne Lamott's *Bird By Bird*, a collection of short essays about the craft of writing by a popular and experienced writer of fiction and nonfiction. Like Elbow, Lamott delivers her advice to writers via personal experience, but Lamott's often irreverent tone helps readers disassociate the kinds of standardized writing many of us experience in school from the kinds of writing professionals do for a living, or just for fun.

These texts, coupled with the assignments I designed for the course (discussed below), come together to present novice teachers of writing with an introduction to composition pedagogy that encourages them to cultivate a critical-pragmatic attitude toward the value of writing as both a pedagogical tool and an outlet for reflection and revision.

Critical Reflection

Without inflating the students' positive evaluations of the course, I believe this approach to English 341 was quite successful. Not only did the course productively engage the advanced composition/composition pedagogy split that I struggled to conceptualize the first couple of times I taught the course, but the students themselves also acknowledged this engagement in their course evaluations and in the retrospective essays I required them to compose at the end of the semester. From my perspective, most of this success was a result of the writing students completed in the course, all of which required them to balance their experienced identity as students with their emerging identity as teachers.

The first essay assignment, which is more or less a literacy narrative, asked students to connect specific moments from their experiences with school to an understanding of what it means to be a teacher. Titled the "Becoming a Teacher" essay, the assignment made explicit reference to Anne Lamott's conversational style of writing in *Bird By Bird*, a book that is constructed around specific memories from the author's life as they relate to the craft of writing. In this way, I asked students to use Lamott's style as a model for imitation to frame their own experiences around whatever ideas about teaching they want to tease out in the essay. Most students wrote about the experience of "playing school" as a child, or they recalled specific teachers from their pasts who influenced their decision to enter the profession. Some students wrote about growing up in a family of teachers, while others discussed their experience being the first person in the family to attend college. In short, this assignment allowed students to identify specific beliefs they hold about the value of teaching while locating where these beliefs originated in their experience.

With the second essay, I asked students to identify and write about a particular experience with failure. Like with the first essay, students were given free reign to write about any experience that was relevant, but herein is where the assignment presented its primary challenge: students could pick a failure from any sphere of their experience. In other words, students did not have to write about a school-based failure, which meant students were also tasked with deciding what counts as "a failure" in the first place. To make this writing even more difficult, the only rule I imposed is that whatever failure students wrote about, they were not allowed to romanticize the failure in their writing by resolving it with a "here's what I learned" or "everything happens for a reason" conclusion. As I told my students, in these essays let the failure be a failure; get it down on the page, shape the narrative as you need to, but don't let the failure turn into anything else. At the time, we were discussing student experiences with composition and the fears and anxieties about writing that sometimes develop early in one's schooling. Peter Elbow's own "failure" essay, "Illiteracy at Harvard and Oxford: Reflections on My Inability to Write," served as a representative example that failure is just as much an idea as it is an occasional result of sometimes arbitrary assessment. Lamott's praise of "shitty first drafts" also conveys a similar attitude about writing: that it is tough to do and doesn't always work out. As Lamott notes, "For me and most of the other writers I know, writing is not rapturous. In fact, the only way I can get anything written is to write really, really shitty first drafts" (22). Writing "shitty first drafts," of course, does not necessarily alleviate the tension inherent in chronicling a personal failure while framing it as such, but this assignment deliberately draws on that tension to mediate the different notions of performance and agency that we bring to the classroom, both as students and teachers. Indeed, as Allison Carr notes in her recent *Composition Forum* article on the subject, "Although we experience and talk about failure in all realms of life, it is especially prominent in our classrooms, where failure is formalized with rubrics and learning outcomes and complicated metrics of assessment" (Carr).

The failure essay was by far the hardest writing students undertook in the course, at least according to them. What stymied most students was the rule I imposed about not resolving whatever failure they chronicle in the essay, which, as my students pointed out, goes against how they are conditioned to think about failure in the first place. For them a failure is a temporary, negative result, one that we learn from in order to produce positive results. Several students wrestled with the concept of failure itself because, according to them, it fell outside the scope of a productive concept. Regardless, this assignment allowed students to interrogate an intimidating concept that often gets used to assess student performance. At the same time they were able to reflect on failure's relative meaning in practice. Because a handful of students wrote about their own failures with writing, moreover, the opportunity to confront these negative associations while doing the very thing at which these students "failed" made for several very interesting and provocative class discussions.

The second half of the semester we turned more explicitly to the work of teaching writing as students tackled the research project I assigned, one I simply dubbed the Praxis Report. My primary goal with the assignment was to show students how to interact with scholarship in a way that might encourage them to use research as a resource in their teaching. To this end, the Praxis Report required students to identify and research a peer-reviewed journal relevant for their area of teaching. After studying back issues of whatever journal they selected, students then had to select several articles from the journal that engaged a topic of interest to them, at least one of which needed to focus on writing in some respect. The report itself (what they submitted to me) consisted of an overview of the selected journal that explains its value for teachers like themselves, three critical summaries that review the articles they selected from the journal, and finally a "praxis" element in which students used what they learned in the articles to craft an assignment sequence, classroom activity, or other practical application to use in their teaching. While students were welcome to freely choose the journal they used for the Praxis Report, I encouraged them to locate journals that were written for practicing teachers, so early-childhood majors might examine *Young Children*, for example, while elementary education majors might select *Language Arts*.

As I discussed in the previous section, one of my initial challenges with the course was figuring out how to teach the teaching of writing to such a wide range of future educators. With the Praxis Report, however, students tackled this issue for themselves by drawing on whatever journal articles they located to articulate what "teaching writing" might look like in the classrooms they are preparing to enter. Reflecting on that assignment now, I can say that altogether students identified pieces of scholarship that interested them and constructed creative applications around this research. In fact, what surprised me the most was how engaged students were with research once they discovered that there are scholarly journals designed for practicing teachers. As a result, I witnessed firsthand future writing teachers wrestle with the untested feasibility of inventing practical applications for pedagogical theory. One student with an interest in physical education, for example, transformed scholarship about the pedagogical value of tracking physical activity into an assignment that requires students to maintain a journal in which they write about how their lifestyle habits reflect whatever health-related concepts they are studying in class. Another student, this one a future third grade teacher, designed a photovoice activity wherein students take portraits of things they enjoy and use the photos to write an autobiography that revolves around their personal interests.

The final writing assignment in English 341 focused on preparing a professional portfolio that contains a resume, job application cover letter, and a teaching philosophy. Locating this assignment at the end of the semester seemed to be a natural fit given the nature of the course; indeed, students welcomed this combination of practical and creative writing as a capstone assignment. Because they had dabbled with several different forms of writing in the class, from nonfiction essay writing to critical summaries of research, students recognized how the professional documents they create to define themselves as teachers should reflect both their personality and their professional experience.

While the course was successful, I do think there are several areas of its design that I should revisit. The primary change I will make with the course is to offer a wider range of readings in composition pedagogy. As I mentioned above, Peter Elbow's *Everyone Can Write* was the primary source I used in this regard, and while several of the essays in this collection directly reflect the thinking I intended my students to connect with their own developing identities as writers and teachers of writing, students were overall resistant to Elbow's work. One reason might be because we used the book almost exclusively during the first half of the semester, when students were initially being introduced to the idea of composition scholarship. Another reason, related to the first, is that Elbow's book is long (it contains over twenty essays) and might intimidate novice teachers of writing. To remedy this problem, I would select only one or two of Elbow's essays and pair them with a handful of other essay-length works that reflect a wider range of voices in composition scholarship. With that said, my students highly enjoyed the Atwell and Newkirk collection, the one book I thought students would resist because of its age, but instead they responded positively to the range of teacher voices in the text. They also enjoyed Lamott's book, especially her use of personal narrative. Perhaps, then, my students were simply resistant to formal, academic writing? This might have been the case, at least until they were given the freedom to choose scholarship themselves to read for the Praxis Report.

In fact the Praxis Report was probably the most useful assignment students completed in the course because it showed them how scholarly resources can be consulted to enhance one's teaching. I did notice, however, that student engagement with this assignment was relative to the appropriateness of the journal they chose to study. While I encouraged students to locate journals that were designed for practicing teachers, I granted leeway, allowing students to use journals intended for scholarly audiences. This was a mistake. At least five to six students in the course selected journals that feature empirical research methodologies, which turned out to be difficult for these non-specialists to process in terms of applicability to their teaching. Despite its importance, research of this nature tends to be produced for fellow specialists and, as such, often relies on jargon-heavy description that is sometimes resistant to narrative interpretation. For example, as one student remarked about *The Journal of Early Childhood Research*, the text she initially selected for the Praxis Report, the articles in this journal are "impossible to follow." The point of the Praxis Report is to show students that engaging, useful research produced for practicing teachers does exist, and it is there for the taking. In the end, those students who selected journals written for specialized scholarly audiences did not have the kind of experience with the Praxis Report as did those students who selected journals written by and for teachers. While I do not want to imply that empirical researchers are not teachers, or that empirical researchers are incapable of writing for non-scholarly audiences, my experience confirms that such research is too complex for students to tackle in the context of English 341, and the Praxis Report assignment in particular.

As I've tried to convey, my approach to the course is rooted in a philosophy of teaching composition that values consequential reflection. One of the hurdles I had to confront was how to teach the teaching of writing to a group of pre-service educators who would be teaching a wide-range of students with vastly different levels of experience. What I did not want to do is design a pedagogy course rooted in current-traditional rhetoric, which, as David Russell reminds us, "sets out to provide students with discrete information and skills, organized systematically, that they can retrieve and apply to any situation requiring communication" (175–76). Moreover, and more to the point, such a course would be practically impossible to undertake because, after all, how does one provide current-traditional writing instruction to a future early childhood teacher that is also relevant for a future middle level math teacher? My attitude had to change and that change was facilitated by adopting a Freirian conception of praxis informed by the values of North American pragmatism, including the belief that instruction is only valuable to the extent that it is useful. In English 341, this method was enacted through course readings, discussions, and writing assignments that challenged students to balance their own experience as writers with questions about and visions for what writing might look like in their future classrooms. Exploring the tensions and anxieties that naturally result from this kind of inquiry is what gives a course like this one its mediating quality, pushing students to think consequently about what they read and write in the course. Indeed, what I've learned from teaching English 341 is that it doesn't matter how a teacher labels her pedagogy or where she locates it within an existing tradition of composition theory, so long as she recognizes that encouraging students to take risks in their writing is what prompts them to internalize the power of writing itself, especially as a resource for engaging the untested feasibility of their learning. In short, it is not enough to construct a pedagogy course that balances theory with practice, especially when we recognize that the best pedagogy courses are the ones in which students harness the power of pragmatic inquiry to transform those limit-situations that encourage us to dichotomize theory and practice from the start.

Works Cited

Carr, Allison. "In Support of Failure." *Composition Forum* 27 (2013): n. pag. Web. 11 February 2013.

Dobrin, Sidney. "Introduction: Finding Space for the Composition Practicum." *Don't Call It That: The Composition Practicum*. Ed. Sidney Dobrin. Urbana: NCTE, 2005. 1–34. Print.

Emig, Janet. "Writing as a Mode of Learning." *CCC* 28.2 (1977): 122–28. Print.

Francis Marion University. *Catalog 2011–12*. Florence, SC: Francis Marion University, 2011. Print.

Freire, Paulo. *Pedagogy of the Oppressed*. 30th Anniversary ed. New York: Continuum, 2006. Print.

Gebhardt, Richard. "Balancing Theory with Practice in the Training of Writing Teachers." *CCC* 28.2 (1977): 134–40. Print.

Knoblauch, C.H., and Lil Brannon. "Writing as Learning Through the Curriculum." *CCC* 45.5 (1983): 465–74. Print.

Lamott, Anne. *Bird By Bird: Some Instructions on Writing and Life*. New York: Anchor, 1995. Print.

Ronald, Kate, and Hephzibah Roskelly. "Untested Feasibility: Imagining the Pragmatic Possibility of Paulo Freire." *College English* 63.5 (2001): 612–32. Print.

Russell, David R. "Vygotsky, Dewey, and Externalism: Beyond the Student/Discipline Dichotomy." *JAC* 13.1 (1993): 173–97. Print.

English 341: Advanced Composition for Teachers

Dr. William Duffy
Founders Hall 110
wduffy@fmarion.edu
Office Hours: MW, 10:30–11:30;
TTH, 1:00–3:00; and by appt.

"Teacher: one who carries on his [or her] education in public."
—Theodore Roethke

Welcome!

This is an advanced writing course designed for future educators and those interested in the vocation of teaching. The two keywords in the name of this course are "advanced" and "teaching," so let me specify what this means for us.

- You are a fairly competent writer who is ready to exert the necessary labor to become a better writer. This means you are committed to pushing yourself into uncomfortable territory that might at times feel exasperating. As well you will seek additional support when needed, especially when suggested by me, your instructor.
- Since this is a 300-level class, you are prepared to be a fully engaged student in the course. There will be a healthy amount of reading and writing, and you should commit to fulfilling the work required of you. Moreover, you are capable of working with others (you do want to be a teacher, after all), so this means you will encourage and respond to one another as the semester proceeds.
- You are nursing an interest in becoming a teacher. Some of you may be wholly committed to such a vocation, while others of you may just be testing the water. Regardless you are ready to devote a semester to thinking, reading, and writing about the work of literacy and learning, especially when it comes to using writing in the classroom.

Course Goals

Each of us brings different experiences to this course as well as different visions about the art of teaching, so part of our work in this class will be to build a community of learners who foster a sense of shared concern. In other words, we are here to learn from one another. In addition, we will tackle the following goals together:

When it comes to teaching…
- To complicate and further our definitions of literacy and how we communicate its personal, academic, and public value.
- To ask questions about and reflect on the role of writing in the work of education, and how to encourage students across grade levels to experiment with and benefit from writing and its challenges.
- To develop strategies for using writing as a method for reflection and discovery in the classroom.

When it comes to (your) writing…
- To build on our existing knowledge of how writing works, as well as how to build productive interventions into each of our unique habits of composing.
- To further our experience as writers aware of the rhetorical and aesthetic dimensions of composing.
- To develop an enhanced appreciation for writing as both an interpretive and productive art, one that affects how we think about, observe, and act in the world around us.

Course Texts

Everyone Can Write by Peter Elbow (Oxford UP)
Bird by Bird by Anne Lamott (Anchor Books)
Understanding Writing by Thomas Newkirk and Nancie Atwell, eds. (Heinemann)

PDFs:

Adams, Marilyn Jager. "Theoretical Approaches to Reading Instruction." *Literacy: A Critical Sourcebook*. Ed. Ellen Cushman, et al. Boston: Bedford/St. Martin's, 2001. 309–15. Print.
Brandt, Deborah. "Sponsors of Literacy." *CCC* 49.2 (1998): 165–85. Print.
Moll, Luis C., and Norma González. "Lessons From Research with Language-Minority Children." *Journal of Reading Behavior* 26.4 (1994): 439–56. Print.

> If you want to be a writer, you must do two things about all others: read a lot and write a lot. There's no way around these two things that I'm aware of, no shortcut.
> —Stephen King

Assignments and Grading

Literacy Narrative	15%
Failure Essay	15%
Praxis Report	20%
Professional Portfolio	25%
Class Citizenship	15%
Mid-term Exam	5%
Final Exam	5%

Course Schedule

Note: UW = *Understanding Writing*

<u>Week 1</u>
Tuesday   Introductions/Review Syllabus
Thursday Read: Matthews, "A Child Composes" (*UW*)

<u>Week 2</u>
Tuesday   Read: Lamott, Introduction and "Getting Started"
Thursday Read: Durst, "Oscar's Journal" (*UW*)

<u>Week 3</u>
Tuesday   Read: Elbow, "Closing My Eyes As I Speak: An Argument for Ignoring Audience" AND Lamott, "Perfectionism"
Thursday Read: Simmons, "The Writer's Chart to Discovery" (*UW*)

<u>Week 4</u>
Tuesday   Full rough draft of Becoming a Teacher Essay due (bring hard-copy)
Thursday Revised version of Becoming a Teacher Essay due

<u>Week 5</u>
Tuesday   Read: Elbow, "Illiteracy at Oxford and Harvard: Reflections on the Inability to Write"
Thursday Read: D'Ambrosio, "Second Graders Can So Write" (*UW*)

Week 6
Tuesday   Read: Elbow, "Freewriting and the Problem of Wheat and Tares" AND Lamott, "Shitty First Drafts"
Thursday   Read: D'Ambrosio, "Second Graders Can So Write" (*UW*)

Week 7
Tuesday   Read: Lamott, "Short Assignments" and "Polaroids" AND Elbow, the three short reflections in "Fragments" section of Part II
            Full rough draft of Failure Essay due
Thursday   Failure Essay Workshop

Week 8
Tuesday   Failure Essay due
Thursday   Read: Bonin, "Beyond Storyland" (*UW*)

Week 9
Tuesday   Read: Elbow, "The War Between Reading and Writing" AND Adams, "Theoretical Approaches to Reading Instruction" (PDF)
Thursday   Read: Moll and González, "Lessons from Research with Language-Minority Children" (PDF)

Week 10
Tuesday   Meet in Library
Thursday   Bring Praxis Report journal articles to class

Week 11
Tuesday   Read: Lamott, "Looking Around" and "Broccoli" AND Elbow, "The Uses of Binary Thinking"
Thursday   Rough drafts of two article summaries due

Week 12
Tuesday   No Class! (Fall Break)
Thursday   Individual Conferences

Week 13
Tuesday   Praxis Report due
Thursday   Read: Brandt, "Sponsors of Literacy" (PDF)

Week 14
Tuesday   Read: Sample teaching philosophies (PDF)
Thursday   No Class! (Thanksgiving Break)

74   Composition Studies

Week 15
Tuesday   Portfolio Workshops
Thursday   Last day of class!
           Professional Portfolio due

Supplemental Materials

On Becoming a Teacher Essay

Description
Throughout this semester, we will be thinking about, studying, and discussing what it means to be a teacher. One of the most important ways to prepare for this vocation is to articulate a sense of what you believe teaching is, why it is important, and how you are coming to construct an identity as a teacher. As the quotation on the top of our course syllabus testifies, a teacher is one who carries on his or her education in public. To this end, the first assignment asks you to do some public articulation via an essay about what you think it means to become a teacher. Your charge is to think hard about why you want to enter the teaching profession. Then, focus on one or two experiences you've had that inform your desire to become a teacher. Tell us about these experiences in a narrative format while also expanding on a belief or two about teaching itself that these experiences have encouraged you to develop. Feel free to imitate Anne Lamott's style of writing in *Bird by Bird*. In particular, study how she uses personal narrative to convey particular lessons or ideas about the vocation of writing in general, but focus your writing (of course) around the vocation of teaching.

Evaluation Criteria
Your "On Becoming a Teacher" essay will be evaluated on the following criteria:
- Your essay focuses on a specific event or experience and details that event or experience in narrative form. In other words, make sure you provide enough details so readers can adequately follow your writing.
- You use whatever event or experience you write about to introduce and expand upon a particular belief or ideal about teaching, one that you believe is important for the teaching profession in general.
- You have organized and edited your essay in a manner that makes it appropriate for a public of your peers. This means the essay is well organized (see models), clearly written, and free of grammar errors.

Failure Essay

Description

The stuff of education involves both successes and failures, hits and misses, trial and error. When it comes to storytelling, and essay writing, the failures are often more interesting and generative than the successes. For this essay, think about a time in your life when you failed and write about it. But don't romanticize this experience; don't spin your writing in terms of a "here's what I learned from this failure" sort of frame. Let your failure be a failure. Don't aim for resolution.

Evaluation Criteria

Your failure essay will be evaluated on the following criteria:
- Building on the skills you practiced in your first essay, you blend narrative composition with reflective writing to shape a well-organized essay that focuses on a singular event that you identify as a failure.
- Within your writing, you convey why this experience can be considered a failure, which will require you to reflect on and define what you consider the idea of "failure" to mean in the first place.
- Your essay has an original title, is at least 1200 words in length, and has been carefully revised and edited for an audience of your peers.

Praxis Report

Description

For the Praxis Report, you will examine recent issues of an academic journal that is relevant to your field of study and locate articles that not only interest you, but also provide informed strategies, theory, advice, etc. for educators like yourself.

There will be several components of your report. They are:
1. An overview of an academic journal of your choice (one that is relevant to you as a teacher) that also includes a summary of your experience reading several of this journal's back issues.
2. Three article responses in which you (1) summarize a specific article from that journal, (2) reflect on its value for you as a teacher, and (3) offer a brief set of 2–4 discussion questions that might spark an engaging conversation with other teachers about the article's topic.
3. A praxis document that outlines and describes one activity, assignment, or other classroom-based practice that you think reflects or builds upon the advice, theory, inquiry or pedagogy, you learned about in at least one of the articles you reviewed.

Evaluation Criteria

Your Praxis Report will be evaluated on the following criteria:

- The introduction to your report not only introduces us to your academic journal (Who sponsors it? Who is its primary audience? What kind of research gets published in it?), but also explains why you selected this journal and why you think it is valuable for a future teacher like yourself.
- In each of your three article reviews you do the following, and in this order: summarize the article, explain why you find this article interesting, and speculate about its potential value for a teacher like yourself.
- Your praxis document clearly outlines and explains a specific classroom-based activity, and you provide a detailed introduction to this activity in which you explain how at least one of the articles you reviewed informs and/or justifies this activity.
- Your final report is consistently formatted, carefully edited, and presented professionally in a folder or small binder (include a title page).

Course Design

English 3135: Visual Rhetoric

Oriana Gatta

As an advanced rhetoric and composition doctoral student, I taught Engl 3135: Visual Rhetoric, a three-credit upper-level course offered by the Department of English at Georgia State University. Mary E. Hocks originally designed this course in 2000 to, in her words, "introduce visual information design theories and practices for writers [and] examine the use of visual meanings in the production of texts, the influence of visual culture on written discourse, and audience-centered document design" ("Undergraduate"). My own research interests include visual rhetoric/culture, feminist theory/pedagogy, critical theory/pedagogy, digital media/pedagogy, and comics studies, and as evidence of the rhet/comp program's deep commitment to graduate student professionalization, I was encouraged to redesign Visual Rhetoric to more specifically reflect these interests. My redesign resulted in a course that employed comics studies as a generative framework on which we built theoretically, historically, and culturally informed definitions of visual rhetoric. Students used these definitions to analyze contemporary popular culture and compose their own research-based arguments in comic book form. To view the course website, please visit: http://criticalrevisions.wordpress.com/.

Institutional Context

Georgia State University is an urban, public, four-year research institution located in downtown Atlanta and has an enrollment of approximately 32,000 students. Its 24,000 or so undergraduates select from among 74 degree programs, and over 100 certificate, MA, and PhD programs are home to approximately 8,000 graduate students. English is one of Georgia State University's largest departments, representing over 500 undergraduates and 300 graduate students. In addition to offering bachelors' degrees in English with emphases in rhetoric and composition, literary studies, creative writing, or secondary English education and graduate (MA, MFA, and PhD) degrees in rhetoric and composition, creative writing, and literary studies, Georgia State University's English department houses Lower Division Studies (the first year composition program), the Writing Studio, and the Writing Across the Curriculum Program, which has also become a division of the recently created Center for Instructional Innovation.

    Rhet/comp faculty played an instrumental role in forming the Second Century Initiative in New and Emerging Media (2CINEM), an interdisciplinary endeavor begun in 2011 to support and develop intellectual and creative innovation within digital media by fostering local, regional, national, and international collaboration among scholars, students, practitioners, and artists. Currently, it is comprised of faculty from the departments of English and communication, and the Ernest G. Welch School of Art & Design, and doctoral fellows from English, communication, and computer science. My course redesign comprised part of the work I completed as a graduate fellow for the 2CINEM's digital pedagogy research group.

The bulk of required undergraduate rhet/comp coursework involves exploring the rhetorical histories, theories, and practices of writing. One required technology-based rhetoric course provides a digital context for this exploration, and to satisfy this requirement, students choose from among five courses, including Technical Writing, Document Design, Electronic Writing and Publishing, Business Writing, and Visual Rhetoric. Students may also take two additional courses from this list to satisfy elective requirements. So, while I could not assume students enrolled in Visual Rhetoric had any level of familiarity with the rhetorical analysis and composition of digital media, I expected them to have working definitions of rhetoric on which we could expand.

Theoretical Rationale

The use of comic books as educational tools in the U.S. has a long, complex history. Between the 1940s and today, approaches to alphabetic literacy, English language acquisition, literary analysis, critical literacy, cultural literacy, visual rhetorical analysis, visual rhetorical composition, and multimodal literacy have at times characterized comics as having pedagogical value. Unfortunately, much of this scholarship approaches comics from the compartmentalizing assumptions that words and images can be easily distinguished from one another and that non-alphabetic images can be more easily apprehended than alphabetic text (e.g., Burmark; George; Hoeness-Krupsaw; Leibold; McCloud, *Understanding*; and Schraffenberger). Similarly, there is a relatively clear-cut division between the analysis and critique of comics as, on the one hand, ideologically imbued cultural artifacts and, on the other, sites of formal design and production. The scholarship employing comics as sites for teaching cultural critique can be further subdivided into those analyzing representations of gender (e.g., Chute, Jonet, and Thalheimer), race/ethnicity (e.g., Chaney, Cong-Huyen and Hong, King, Nama, Rifas, Strömberg, and Wanzo), and sexuality (e.g., Van Dyne), respectively. For composition studies, a field invested in understanding and developing our students' and our own abilities to communicate in complex, multiple, and intersecting historical, cultural, and social contexts, it is counterproductive to take a "separate but equal" approach to visual and verbal texts and their analysis, production, and ideology

I am not the first to make this claim. Work done by feminist, digital, and rhetorical theorists such as Hocks, Anne Francis Wysocki, and Cheryl E. Ball, particularly in relation to new media and multimodal and digital composition, emphasizes the interrelationship of analysis and composition. Hocks, Wysocki, and Ball, drawing in part on the work of the New London Group, use the framework of "design" to discuss both formal construction and the sets of assumptions or ideologies—such as those that dichotomize images and text, analysis and composition, and even rhetoric and ideology—that shape a composer's decisions and contextualize an audience's reception. They argue that the extent to which we can facilitate our students' awareness and understanding of these assumptions is the extent to which we enable them to be more conscious consumers and, even more importantly, rhetorically savvy composers of culture. Their work therefore parallels and extends a critical pedagogical approach to composition that requires acknowledging the rhetorical construction of ideology.

Further, as critical theorist Roland Barthes points out, ideologies function in culture at the meta-narrative level, persuading us through repetition to accept the values they indirectly imply, often through stories. Feminist scholar AnaLouise Keating labels these "status quo stories," stories told and retold to "normalize and naturalize the existing social systems, values, and norms so entirely that [we] deny the possibility of change" (23). As such, teaching students how to analyze narratives has become a common practice at all levels of visual rhetorical education. And as visual narratives, comics have increasingly been used to identify and critique representations of oppressive ideologies of gender, race, sexuality, nationality, and to a lesser extent, class (e.g., Chaney, Dong, King, and Thalheimer).

Despite this analytical investment, and like multimodal composing more generally (Palmeri), much of the advocacy for and engagement in composing comics occurs in elementary and high school contexts (e.g., Bitz; Carter; Lamb and Johnson), and most of the work written about composing comics in undergraduate writing classrooms does not address the intersection of rhetorical construction and ideological meaning, nor the opportunities that comics provide for challenging oppressive ideological perspectives (e.g., Carter, Frey and Fisher, and Haendiges). An exception is Wysocki and Dennis A. Lynch's *Compose, Design, Advocate: A Rhetoric for Integrating Written, Visual, and Oral Communication*, which advocates an embodied approach to the rhetorical analysis and composition of comics (510). In one chapter, "Analyzing Comics," Wysocki and Lynch argue that students can enact an embodied understanding of comics' rhetorical construction by drawing on their individually as well as historically and culturally situated experiences. Employing two well-known texts, the "Common Scents" chapter in Lynda Barry's *One! Hundred! Demons!* and Marjane Satrapi's *Persepolis*, Wysocki and Lynch lead students through the rhetorical analytical work of exploring the relationships among authorial purpose, genre, alphabetic texts, visual styles, authors' self-representations, representations of family, representations of experience, and students' experiences. Wysocki and Lynch then invite students to begin composing their own comic narratives using the rhetorical structures students identify.

My pedagogical approach to Visual Rhetoric expands on Wysocki and Lynch's work by making the rhetorical analysis of visual culture and the rhetorical composition of comic (or sequential) narratives the course's primary foci. In doing so, I aimed to (1) expand definitions of composition beyond alphabetic texts, (2) identify the rhetorical significance of genre conventions and the media through which they are expressed, (3) highlight narrative and metanarrative intersections, (4) explore comics as examples of multigenre, multimedia narrativity, and (5) help students compose original, research-based arguments in comic form on some aspect of contemporary popular culture to demonstrate a nuanced understanding of visual rhetoric. These goals formed a rough trajectory for the coursework.

To begin building students' vocabulary for and understanding of rhetoric, including and beyond alphabetic images, we began with Ball and Kristin L. Arola's *visualizing composition 2.0*, which offers definitions and analytical exercises for several visual rhetorical elements (e.g., color, contrast, alignment, organization, etc.) exemplified by both student-produced and professional work. These terms became the first items on the list of analytical criteria we explored and further developed throughout the semester. While completing Ball and Arola's analytical exercises, we also read and discussed the second chapter of Scott McCloud's *Understanding Comics: The Invisible Art* to contextualize visual rhetoric in relation to comics. Additionally, *Understanding Comics* functioned as an example of the kind of work I was looking for in students' final projects: a sequential narrative exploration of how the topic of interest has been (visually) represented and understood and what we should (not) think/do about that representation and understanding.

We read Stephen Greenblatt's "Culture" essay, the first three chapters of John Berger's *Ways of Seeing*, and Wysocki's "The Sticky Embrace of Beauty: On Some Formal Relations in Teaching about the Visual Aspects of Texts" to begin considering in what ways still and moving images in different genres and media communicate cultural values. Though Greenblatt is primarily concerned with literary criticism, his claim that art is a conduit for "the roles by which men and women are expected to pattern their lives" did a good job of introducing a connection between aesthetics and culture (228). Berger's work shifts the analytical focus from literature to painting and offers numerous examples of the gendered and classed assumptions underlying genre-based, artistic practices. Focusing on a print *Peek* magazine advertisement, Wysocki points out that the separation of form and content in design principles assumes the possibility of an objective assessment of an image's aesthetic value without regard to how aesthetic values are culturally constructed and, in this case, gendered. Consequently, we added "values," "genre," "medium," "symbolism," "bodies/embodiment," "gender," "race," "class," "age," "sexuality," "strangeness," and "absence" to our growing list of analytical criteria during class discussions of these texts.

Shifting our focus from analysis to production and the more serious consideration of research topics for students' final projects, we read the introductory chapter of Henry Jenkins' *Convergence Culture: Where Old and New Media Collide* and volume one of Mike Carey and Peter Gross' *The Unwritten* comic book series. Both texts foreground the increasingly blurry distinction between producers and consumers of (digital) culture, the opportunities (digital) media provide to both support and challenge a given status quo, and the rhetorical function of intertexuality in contemporary (digital) culture. Additionally, while we consistently drew parallels between contemporary digital culture and genres of print culture, Jenkins' work foregrounded digital production and consumption, and *The Unwritten* functioned as another example of the kind of work I expected students to compose for their final projects: sequential narratives that examine and enact the rhetorical construction of ideology in popular culture.

Students submitted topic proposals after this series of readings and, to gain research experience in multiple media(ted) contexts, they completed digital collages and annotated bibliographies based on these proposals. For the collages, I asked students to (1) select still and moving images that represented various perspectives on their topics (e.g., internet memes, film clips, magazine covers, billboards, etc.), (2) use the visual rhetorical analytical criteria we had thus far identified (e.g., relating to use of color, contrast, emphasis, bodies/embodiment, absence, symbolism, values, etc.) to identify the rhetorical moves at work and to assess the value of these moves to the students' projects, and (3) upload and arrange their digitized images in Prezi as a collage that makes an argument regarding the selected images' visual rhetorical effectiveness. For example, one student researching the relationship between Apple's software marketing and technological innovation juxtaposed images from Apple's "I'm a Mac and I'm a PC" advertising campaign with infographics on Unix-based operating systems to point out how effectively Apple has promoted its products by constructing a binary opposition between "young," "cool," and "cutting-edge" Mac OS X and "old," "ugly," "unreliable" Windows. This student found that one effect of the binary is to neglect the plethora of comparable (and open-source) operating systems. The collage assignment served as a starting point for students' research projects by familiarizing them with multiple perspectives on their topics. Students then completed annotated bibliographies, consisting of articles from scholarly publications, to further engage the complexities of their topics.

To focus specifically on the rhetorical choices, including "moment," "frame," "image," "word," and "flow," available in constructing sequential narratives, we read the first chapter of McCloud's *Making Comics: Storytelling Secrets of Comics, Manga, and Graphic Novels* (10). Additionally, though I did not require students to use any of these options, we experimented with several digital formats for composing comics, including *Comic Life*, *ToonDoo*, *BitStrips*, and *Pixton*, so that students could assess the affordances of each in relation to other available means such as hand-drawn images. For the remainder of the course, students workshopped drafts, presented finished narratives, and composed written rhetorical analyses of these narratives in which they contextualized their understanding of visual rhetoric in relation to their own work.

Critical Reflection

Students' final projects and analyses speak to their level of success mastering course content: their intentional adaptation of the genre conventions characteristic of the aspects of contemporary popular culture they researched demonstrate their ability to engage in historically and culturally nuanced rhetorical analysis and composition that acknowledges and challenges the use-value of a text/image distinction and enacts the relationship between form and (ideological) content. For example, a student exploring (mis) representations of Zen in contemporary Western culture juxtaposed the minimalist aesthetic characteristic of superficial representations of Zen—including basic forms, a watercolor technique, and a black-and-white color scheme—with one character's use of Zen koans, or riddles, to challenge any simplistic definition of Zen. A student exploring the relationship between celebrity worship and religious human sacrifice employed several visual references to classic horror films to underline the connection between what we see and how we see. And a student exploring webcomics' creative impact on the definition(s) of comics made a webcomic that offered an expanded definition to a skeptical audience.

According to informal feedback, students attested to their expanded definitions of composition, citing the sequential narrative assignment as a catalyst for moving beyond traditional academic essays. Students also said the rhetorical analysis of real-world cultural artifacts made the visual rhetorical subject matter more comprehensible, and the assignment scaffolding and option to revise most assignments made learning course content easier. These perspectives help validate using comics studies as a frame through which to teach visual rhetorical analysis and composition. They also suggest that analysis is a useful scaffold for production.

As validating as these perspectives are, the course did not play out exactly as I had anticipated, and there are several aspects of the course I would alter. While Ball and Arola's *visualizing composition 2.0* is an invaluable resource and starting point for discussing formal elements of visual rhetoric, I think students would become more quickly engaged in the subject matter were they to identify and present their own examples of these elements rather than use Ball and Arola's examples for all of the analytical exercises, or even construct their own list of terms, definitions, and examples to which they could compare Ball and Arola's work. Wysocki makes this point in the "Design Analysis" assignment she offers as an extension of her work problematizing formal design categories ("Sticky Embrace" 181).

Beyond employing a more student-centered, inductive versus deductive approach to knowledge creation characteristic of feminist and critical composition pedagogies, generating their own elements of visual rhetoric would also give students another opportunity to discuss audience, as they would need to consider the appeal of their terms, definitions, and examples in relation to their classmates as audience members. Along these same lines, the course lacked more direct conversations about the relationship between students' target audiences and potential sites for disseminating their sequential narratives. These conversations would also allow us to address students' choices of digital composing tools and the extent to which the options and constraints of each match up with students' skill levels, their audience's familiarity with comics, and the visual conventions comics employ.

Citing the creative limitations of any one medium of production, most students employed some combination of print and digital design tools to compose their final projects. These choices demonstrate students' rhetorical intentionality. They also highlight the necessity for recognizing and addressing the multimodality of visual rhetorical praxis. Jody Shipka argues that "*all* communicative practice," not just digital media, is multimodal based on "the roles other texts, talk, people, perceptions, semiotic resources, technologies, motives, activities, and institutions play in the production, reception, circulation, and valuation of seemingly stable finished texts" (13, emphasis in original). Further, using cognitive scientist Patrick Colm Hogan's work as grounds for composition studies' more serious engagement in the interdisciplinary study of creativity, Jason Palmeri argues, "composers are better able to make remote associations if they draw upon and combine multiple creative traditions" (31). Accordingly, in future iterations of this course, a more direct framing of comic production as *multimodal* composition, and the print and digital genres and media we analyze as historically and culturally dependent *modes* of communication may increase students' ability to transfer their rhetorical skills from one communicative, (inter)disciplinary context to another.

Works Cited

Ball, Cheryl E. "Designerly [does not equal] Readerly: Re-Assessing Multimodal and New Media Rubrics for Use in Writing Studies." *Convergence: The International Journal of Research into New Media Technologies*. 12.4 (2006): 393–412. Print.

Barthes, Roland. *Mythologies*. New York: Hill and Wang, 1972. Print.

Bitz. Michael. *When Commas Meet Kryptonite: Classroom Lessons from The Comic Book Project*. New York: Teachers College P, 2010. Print.

Burmark, Lynell. "Visual Literacy: What You Get is What You See." *Teaching Visual Literacy: Using Comic Books, Graphic Novels, Anime, Cartoons, and More to Develop Comprehension and Thinking Skills*. Ed. Nancy Frey and Douglas Fisher. Thousand Oaks, CA: Corwin P, 2008. 5–25. Print.

Carter, James Bucky, ed. *Building Literacy Connections with Graphic Novels: Page by Page, Panel by Panel*. Urbana, IL: NCTE, 2006. 1–25. Print.

Chaney, Michael A. "Is There an African American Graphic Novel?" *Teaching the Graphic Novel*. Ed. Stephen E. Tabachnick. New York: MLA, 2009. 69–75. Print.

Chute, Hillary. *Graphic Women: Life Narratives and Contemporary Comics*. New York: Columbia UP, 2010. Print.

Cong-Huyen, Anne, and Caroline Kyungah Hong. "Teaching Asian-American Graphic Narratives in a 'Post-Race' Era." *Teaching Comics and Graphic Narratives: Essays on Theory, Strategy and Practice*. Ed. Lan Dong. Jefferson, NC: McFarland, 2012. 80–93. Print.

Dong, Lan, ed. *Teaching Comics and Graphic Narratives: Essays on Theory, Strategy and Practice*. Jefferson, NC: McFarland, 2012. Print.

Frey, Nancy, and Douglas Fisher, eds. *Teaching Visual Literacy: Using Comic Books, Graphic Novels, Anime, Cartoons, and More to Develop Comprehension and Thinking Skills*. Thousand Oaks, CA: Corwin P, 2008. Print.

George, Diana. "From Analysis to Design: Visual Communication in the Teaching of Writing." *CCC* 54.1 (2002): 11–39. Print.

Greenblatt, Stephen. "Culture." *Critical Terms for Literary Studies*. Ed. Frank Lentricchia and Thomas McLaughlin. Chicago: U of Chicago P, 1989. 225–32. Print.

Haendiges, J. A. *Mobility and the Digital Page*. Diss. Washington State University, 2010. Ann Arbor: *ProQuest*. Web. 31 May 2011.

Hocks, Mary E. "Visual Rhetoric in Digital Writing Environments." *CCC* 54.4 (2003): 629–56. Print.

Hoeness-Krupsaw, Susanna. "Ivorian Bonus: Teaching Abouet and Oubrerie's *Aya*." *Teaching Comics and Graphic Narratives: Essays on Theory, Strategy, and Practice*. Ed. Lan Dong. Jefferson, NC: McFarland, 2012. 161–72. Print.

Jonet, M. Catherine. "Our Graphics, Ourselves: Graphic Narratives and the Gender Studies Classroom." *Teaching Comics and Graphic Narratives: Essays on Theory, Strategy, and Practice*. Ed. Lan Dong. Jefferson, NC: McFarland, 2012. 119–29. Print.

Keating, AnaLouise. *Teaching Transformation: Transcultural Classroom Dialogues*. New York: Palgrave, 2007. Print.

King, C. Richard. "Envisioning Justice: Racial Metaphors, Political Movements, and Critical Pedagogy." *Writing the Visual: A Practical Guide for Teachers of Composition and Communication.* Ed. Carol David and Anne E. Richards. New York: Parlor, 2008. 87–104. Print.

Lamb, Annette, and Larry Johnson. "Graphic Novels, Digital Comics, and Technology Enhanced Learning: Part 2." *Teacher Librarian* 36.1 (2009): 70–75. Print.

Leibold, Don. "Abandon Every Fear, Ye That Enter: The X-Men Journey through Dante's *Inferno*." *Building Literacy Connections with Graphic Novels: Page by Page, Panel by Panel.* Ed. James Bucky Carter. Urbana, IL: NCTE, 2007. 100–12. Print.

McCloud, Scott. *Making Comics: Storytelling Secrets of Comics, Manga, and Graphic Novels.* New York: Harper, 2006. Print.

—. *Understanding Comics: The Invisible Art.* New York: Harper Perennial, 1993. Print.

Nama, Adilifu. *Super Black: American Pop Culture and Black Superheroes.* Austin: U of Texas P, 2011. Print.

Palmeri, Jason. *Remixing Composition: A History of Multimodal Writing Pedagogy.* Carbondale, IL: SIUP, 2012. Print.

Rifas, Leonard. "Race and Comics." *Multicultural Comics: From* Zap *to* Blue Beetle. Ed. Frederick Luis Aldama. Austin: U of Texas P, 2010. 27–38. Print.

Schraffenberger, J.D. "Vizualizing Beowulf: Old English Gets Graphic." *Building Literacy Connections with Graphic Novels: Page by Page, Panel by Panel.* Ed. James Bucky Carter. Urbana, IL: NCTE, 2007. 64–82. Print.

Shipka, Jody. *Toward a Composition Made Whole.* Pittsburgh: U of Pittsburgh P, 2011. Print.

Strömberg, Fredrik. *Black Images in the Comics: A Visual History.* Seattle, WA: Fantagraphics, 2003. Print.

Thalheimer, Anne N. "Too Weenie to Deal with All of this 'Girl Stuff': Women, Comics and the Classroom." *Teaching the Graphic Novel.* Ed. Stephen Tabachnick. New York: MLA, 2009. 84–90. Print.

"Undergraduate Courses." *Rhetoric and Composition.* Georgia State University. n.d. Web. 5 Aug. 2013.

Wanzo, Rebecca. "Black Nationalism, Bunraku, and Beyond: Articulating Black Heroism through Cultural Fusion and Comics." *Multicultural Comics: From* Zap *to* Blue Beetle. Ed. Frederick Luis Aldama. Austin: U of Texas P, 2010. 93–104. Print.

Welhausen, Candice. *Toward a Visual Paideia: Visual Rhetoric in Undergraduate Writing Programs.* Diss. U of New Mexico, 2009. Ann Arbor: *ProQuest.* Web. 31 May 2011.

Wysocki, Anne Frances. "awaywithwords: On the possibilities in unavailable designs." *Computers and Composition* 22 (2005): 55–62. Print.

—. "The Sticky Embrace of Beauty: On Some Formal Problems of Teaching about the Visual Aspects of Texts." *Writing New Media: Theory and Applications for Expanding the Teaching of Composition.* Logan, UT: Utah State UP, 2004. 147–98. Print.

Wysocki, Anne Frances, and Dennis A. Lynch. *Compose, Design, Advocate: A Rhetoric for Integrating Written, Visual, and Oral Communication.* New York: Pearson/Longman, 2007. Print.

(Re)visions: A Critically Comic Approach to Visual Rhetoric

"I remember standing on a street corner with the black painter Beuford Delaney down in the Village, waiting for the light to change, and he pointed down and said, Look. I looked and all I saw was water. And he said, Look again, which I did, and I saw oil on the water and the city reflected in the puddle. It was a great revelation to me. I can't explain it. He taught me how to see, and how to trust what I saw. Painters have often taught writers how to see. And once you've had that experience, you see differently."

—James Baldwin, "The Art of Fiction,"
The Paris Review Interviews, Vol. II

"Really, what changes the world is the power of a compelling story. But we seem to carefully limit the stories that reach us to those that won't push us to change."

—Elana Dykewomon, "The Body Politic: Mediations on Identity,"
This Bridge We Call Home

"As an experienced screenwriter told me, 'When I first started, you would pitch a story because without a good story, you didn't really have a film. Later, once sequels started to take off, you pitched a character because a good character could support multiple stories. And now, you pitch a world because a world can support multiple characters and multiple stories across multiple media'."

—Henry Jenkins, *Convergence Culture:
Where Old and New Media Collide*

"Design gives students' work social and political impact and allows them to learn how to represent new forms of knowledge. To establish a balanced rhetorical approach, then, we must offer students experiences both in the analytic process of critique, which scrutinizes conventional expectations and power relations, and in the transformative process of design, which can change power relations by creating a new vision of knowledge. In terms of visual rhetoric, students need to learn the 'distanced' process of how to critique the saturated visual and technological landscape that surrounds them as something structured and written in a set of deliberate rhetorical moves."

—Mary Hocks, "Visual Rhetoric in Digital Writing Environments," *College Composition and Communication*

Course Description

Visual Rhetoric introduces visual design theories and practices for writers and explores the relationship among visual rhetoric, digital media, and contemporary culture. More specifically, this course examines the rhetorical construction and use of visual meanings in media production via (1) blogged responses to and class discussion of assigned readings, (2) audience-centered analysis of digital media designed by others, and (3) work with digital communication and software tools to produce a sequential narrative incorporating research that addresses the influence of visual media in contemporary popular/mass culture.

Course Goals

- Understand the uses of visuals for persuasive purposes and in multiple media.
- Understand the impact of visuals on digital communication.
- Practice visual rhetoric with and for an audience.
- Connect visual rhetoric with rhetorical theory, composition strategies, and technology.

Course Outcomes

By the successful completion of this course, students will be able to:
- Describe relationships among words, images, and various visual media.
- Identify the major rhetorical elements of self- and other-composed designs.
- Analyze and evaluate the rhetorical success or failure of a design in terms of its audience, meanings, and intended effect.
- Apply rhetorical principles in the digital production of visual media.

Required Online Access

Ball, Cheryl E., and Kristin L. Arola. *visualizing composition 2.0*. Boston: Bedford/St. Martins, 2010. Web. Purchase online access here: http://bcs.bedfordstmartins.com/rewriting2e/default.asp#t_616472____

Required Book-Length Texts

Kul-Want, Christopher, and Piero. *Introducing Aesthetics: A Graphic Guide*. London: Icon, 2010. Print.

Carey, Mike, and Peter Gross. *Unwritten Vol. 1: Tommy Taylor and the Bogus Identity*. New York: Vertigo, 2010. Print.

Additional Required Readings and Materials

Note that all of these texts are available online (via the Georgia State University Library website or the Internet in general), so *no purchase is necessary*. Additionally, we will not be reading any of the book-length works in full, so this reading list is not as massive as it might first appear.

Berger, John. *Ways of Seeing*. London: Penguin, 1972. Print.

Greenblatt, Stephen. "Culture." *Critical Terms for Literary Studies*. Ed. Frank Lentricchia and Thomas McLaughlin. Chicago: U of Chicago P, 1989. 225–32. Print.

Jenkins, Henry. *Convergence Culture: When Old and New Media Collide*. New York: NYU P, 2006. Print.

McCloud, Scott. *Understanding Comics: The Invisible Art*. New York: Harper Paperbacks, 1994. Print.

Rifas, Leonard. "Educational Comics." *Encyclopedia of Comic Books and Graphic Novels*. Ed. M. Keith Booker. Westport, CT: Greenwood, 2010. 160–69. Print.

Wysocki, Anne Frances. "The Sticky Embrace of Beauty: On Some Formal Problems of Teaching about the Visual Aspects of Texts." *Writing New Media: Theory and Applications for Expanding the Teaching of Composition*. Logan, UT: Utah State UP, 2004. 147–98. Print.

*High-capacity digital storage media such as a USB drive must be used to save all of your work. Access to email, the Web, and printing capabilities, whether from home, work, or a campus lab.

Assignments

Note that the assignment descriptions offered below are brief overviews. Full-length assignment sheets that include requirements, due date(s), and evaluation criteria will be posted to the class website (http://criticalrevisions.wordpress.com/coursework) and discussed in class.

Blogging (20%, 200 pts.)

Everyone will create his or her own blog using Wordpress online software. Consider your blog as a visual rhetorical expression of your identity and your understanding of/relationship to visual rhetoric. Each week you will post written responses to required readings on these blogs. Additionally, your blog will serve as an archive for the research you complete related to your final project.

Evaluation Criteria

As there is no pre-defined number of required posts, assessment will be based in part (150 pts.) on the percentage of posts completed (including a final post that describes and analyzes the visual rhetorical choices you made in designing your blog). This percentage will be calculated by dividing the number of posts you've completed by the total number of assigned posts. For example, if you completed 25 posts, and there were 27 total posts assigned, you would receive an A (93% /139.5 pts.).

The other part (50 pts.) will be assessed based on the following criteria:
- 20 pts: Evidence of rhetorical decision-making related to your blog URL, title, and theme.
- 10 pts: Creation of an "About" page describing yourself and your relationship to/understanding of visual rhetoric.
- 10 pts: Creation of post categories related to your final project.
- 10 pts: Creation of links and link categories related to your final project.

The overall grade for the blogging assignment will be calculated by adding the total number of points earned from your blog posts and blog design and dividing this number by the total possible number of points (200). For example, if you did 25 of 27 posts, and received 50 points for your blog design, your overall grade would be an A (95%/189.5 pts.).

Sequential Narrative Topic Proposal (10%, 100 pts.)
The topic proposal, in which you identify and explain your topic of choice, is the first step towards completing your sequential narrative.

Evaluation Criteria

Your proposal will be assessed based on your inclusion, or lack, of the required elements noted below.
- 15 points: Genre identification(s)
- 15 points: Example text identification(s)
- 15 points: Significance
- 15 points: Tentative claim/hypothesis
- 15 points: Formal tone and linguistic clarity
- 15 points: Length requirement (250–300 words)
- 10 points: Format requirement (MLA)

Sequential Narrative Topical Collage Prezi and Rhetorical Analysis (20%, 200 pts.)

Everyone will be introduced to Prezi presentation software. Using this software, you will create and present a visual collage (10%, 100 pts.), or "remix," of ten still and/or moving images that relate to the topic you have chosen for your final project with the goal of identifying a visual rhetorical approach (or approaches) to your sequential narrative. Additionally, you will submit a written comparative rhetorical analysis of the images in your collage and your "remixing" of them.

Evaluation Criteria

Your proposal will be assessed based on your inclusion, or lack thereof, of the required elements noted below.

Visual Collage:
- 10 points: Ten different images used.
- 50 points: Visual rhetorical construction that points to/suggests explanations for how and why the images you have selected are visually rhetorically in/effective.
- 10 points: No fewer than five and no more than six minutes spent presenting your topical collage to the class.

Comparative Analysis Essay:
- 10 points: Ten different still/moving images discussed.
- 10 points: Clear thesis statement regarding the visual/rhetorical in/effectiveness of the images you have selected.
- 50 points: Evidence in support of your argument, i.e., clear and detailed explanations for how and why the images you have selected are visually rhetorically in/effective based on the analytical criteria we have discussed in class.
- 30 points: Explanation of why the decisions you made in constructing your Prezi make it visually rhetorically effective.
- 10 points: Formal tone and linguistic clarity.
- 10 points: Correct MLA format (including Works Cited page) in comparative analysis essay.
- 10 points: Citations on the Works Cited page for each image used.

Sequential Narrative Annotated Bibliography (10%, 100 pts.)

Constructing an effective argument, visual or otherwise, requires research. In order to gain a deeper understanding of your topic and the evidence for (and against) your argument, you will complete a five-to-eight source annotated bibliography. Three of these sources must be scholarly (see the "Resources" page for a refresher on identifying scholarly sources).

Evaluation Criteria

- 30 points: Three scholarly sources.
- 10 points: At least five sources total.
- 10 points: A sentence in each annotation describing the source's claim.
- 10 points: A sentence in each annotation describing the source's evidence in support of the claim.
- 10 points: A sentence in each annotation describing the purpose of the source's argument.
- 10 points: A sentence in each annotation describing the source's audience.
- 10 points: A sentence in each annotation describing the use-value of the source in relation to your project.
- 10 points: Correct MLA formatting.

Sequential Narrative Three-Minute Work-In-Progress Report (5%, 50 pts.)
You will write a one-to-two page report detailing your progress thus far and the additional work you intend to do to complete your sequential narrative. In order to receive feedback from your classmates and instructor on your sequential narrative, you will briefly present this information to the class.

Evaluation Criteria

- 10 points: A description of the progress you have made thus far.
- 10 points: A description of the additional work you intend to do to complete your project.
- 10 points: A description of the issues/concerns you still need to work out in order to complete your project.
- 10 points: At least one page in length (not including nameplate).
- 10 points: Correct MLA formatting.

Sequential Narrative (15%, 150 pts.)
Building on all you have learned about visual rhetoric, design conventions, and sequential narrative in the first half of the course, and based on scholarly research about a topic related to course material, you will create your own sequential narrative in comic book form. The purpose of this narrative will be to make an argument regarding some aspect of contemporary visual culture.

Evaluation Criteria

- 20 points: At least 50 frames (for a comic strip or webcomic) or 8 pages (for a comic book).
- 30 points: Visual rhetorical construction clearly evidences a target audience.
- 40 points: Visual rhetorical construction clearly evidences a claim, i.e., something you
- want your audience to think and/or do.
- 20 points: Visual rhetorical construction clearly evidences a purpose, i.e., why you want
- your target audience to think and/or do what your claim encourages them to.
- 30 points: Visual rhetorical construction offers clear evidence in support of your claim.
- 10 points: Visual rhetorical construction clearly acknowledges at least one alternative perspective on the topic your narrative addresses.

Sequential Narrative Rhetorical Analysis Essay (10%, 100 pts.)
You will write a four-to-five page essay explaining the (visual) rhetorical choices you made in constructing your sequential narrative and how these choices relate to your argument. This essay should also include a Works Cited page listing all of the visual, verbal, print, and digital texts you used in constructing your narrative.

Evaluation Criteria

- 10 points: Length of at least four pages, not including the Works Cited page.
- 10 points: An introduction that describes your topic and identifies the argument you intend your sequential narrative to make.
- 10 points: A thesis statement that evaluates the effectiveness of the argument you present in your sequential narrative based on the visual rhetorical criteria we have generated in class (and which are listed on the "Analytical Criteria" page of the class website).
- 30 points: Evidence in support of your thesis statement, i.e., clear and detailed descriptions of the choices you made in composing your sequential narrative and explanations of why these choices are visually rhetorically effective based on the criteria you identify in your thesis statement.
- 10 points: A conclusion that identifies any alterations you would make to your sequential narrative given more time and why you would make these changes.

- 10 points: Formal Tone and Linguistic Clarity.
- 10 points: Correct MLA formatting (including Works Cited page).
- 10 points: Citations on the Works Cited page for each source (including images) used.

8–10 minute Sequential Narrative Presentation (10%, 100 pts.)
You will present your completed sequential narrative to class, including explanations you offered in your rhetorical analysis essay for your (visual) rhetorical choices and their relationship to your argument.

Evaluation Criteria

- 10 points: Used images of your sequential narrative to exemplify each of the points you make about its visual rhetorical effectiveness.
- 10 points: Addressed the visual rhetorical construction of sequential narrative's target audience.
- 10 points: Addressed the visual rhetorical construction of sequential narrative's claim.
- 10 points: Addressed the visual rhetorical construction of sequential narrative's purpose.
- 10 points: Addressed the visual rhetorical construction of sequential narrative's evidence.
- 10 points: Addressed the visual rhetorical construction of sequential narrative's alternative perspective(s).
- 10 points: Coherently articulated ideas.
- 10 points: Employed digital presentation media.
- 10 points: Engaged and maintained audience's attention.
- 10 points: Spent no fewer than eight minutes and no more than ten minutes presenting.

Course Schedule

To view the complete course schedule, please visit: http://criticalrevisions.wordpress.com/schedule.

Week 1: "In a World . . ."
Reading: Review the class website.
Writing: Email me (oriana.gatta@gmail.com) with responses to the following questions:

- What, if any, questions do you have about the course based on your review of the course website?
- Why are you taking this course?
- What are your goals for this course?

- What are your career/life goals?
- What image would you choose to describe yourself or one of your interests? (*Add as an email attachment)

Week 2: A Formal/Cultural Introduction to Visual Rhetoric
Reading: *Understanding Comics* Chapter 2 (Access on the Resources page of this blog, under "Required Readings" and *visualizing composition 2.0*)

Writing: Post your responses to the questions at the end of the of each *visualizing composition 2.0* module on your own blogs.

Week 3: Seeing Culture
Reading: Wysocki's "Sticky Embrace of Beauty," Stephen Greenblatt's "Culture," and John Berger's *Ways of Seeing*, Ch. 1 & 3

Writing
- In a post to the class blog, identify at least three criteria Wysocki uses to analyze the *Peek* advertisement, and use these criteria to analyze an advertisement of your own choosing. Make sure to include an image of the advertisement you select and/or a link to it (if it is a moving image) in your post.
- Using your previously selected advertisement, answer in a blog post the six questions for critical analysis proposed by Greenblatt.

Week 4: Sequential Culture
Reading: Henry Jenkins' Introduction to *Convergence Culture,* Leonard Rifas' "Educational Comics," and Mike Carey and Peter Gross's *Unwritten Vol. 1: Tommy Taylor and the Bogus Identity*

Writing
- Post an original example of cultural convergence as defined by Jenkins to your blog and explain why it works as an example.
- In a post on your blog, identify at least one parallel between Carey and Gross's story and contemporary culture, and using at least two themes (visually and/or verbally recurring elements) in *Unwritten* Vol. 1, explain a possible argument Carey and Gross might be making about the aspect of contemporary culture paralleled in their comic book.

Week 5: Sequential Culture, Continued.
Reading: *Introducing Aesthetics: A Graphic Guide.*
Writing
- In a post on your blog, identify at least two themes (visually and/or verbally recurring elements) in *Introducing Aesthetics*, and explain a pos-

sible argument Kul-Want and Piero may be making about aesthetics using these themes.
- Using the post title "Unabridged Topic Ideas," post all of your potential topic ideas to your blog. Read through at least three of your classmates' topic ideas, and comment on these three with at least one comment and/or question.

Week 6: Hot Topics
Reading: Go to http://prezi.com/learn/ and watch "Get Started," "Go to the Next Level," and "Share Your Prezi."

Due: Critical Reflection Essay and Topic Proposal

Week 7: Work It!
Writing: Begin working on Topical Collage Prezi.

Week 8: Topical Collage Prezi Presentations
Writing: Continue working on Topical Collage Prezi.

Due: Topic Proposal Revisions, Topical Collage Prezi, and Comparative Analysis Essay

Week 9: Topical Collage Prezi Presentations, Continued
Reading: Margaret K. Woodworth's "The Rhetorical Precis" and secondary source you located.

Writing: Write a rhetorical precis of secondary source and post it to your blog.

Week 10: Work It (Reprise)!
Reading: Another source located for your annotated bibliography.

Writing: Write a rhetorical precis of another source and post it to your blog.

Week 11: Commence Sequential Narratives
Reading: Chapter 1 of Scott McCloud's *Making Comics*.

Writing: On your own blog, post a description of at least three similarities between McCloud's characterization of comic composition and the elements of visual rhetoric we have thus far identified.

Due: Annotated bibliography.

Week 12: Continue Sequential Narratives
Writing
- On your own blog, post a 250–300 word description of your sequential narrative as you've thus far conceptualized it.

- On your blog, post a piece of your actual sequential narrative, i.e., a frame, series of frames, character representation, setting representation, etc. for feedback.

Week 13: Sequential Narrative Progress Reports
Due: Sequential Narrative Work-in-Progress Report

Week 14: Break it Down
Thanksgiving Break

Week 15: Sequential Narrative Presentations
Due: Sequential Narratives

Week 16: Sequential Narrative Presentations, Continued
Due: Sequential Narrative Rhetorical Analyses

Book Reviews

Writing Studies Research in Practice: Methods and Methodologies, edited by Lee Nickoson and Mary P. Sheridan. Carbondale and Edwardsville: SIUP, 2013. 289 pp.

Reviewed by Amanda Athon, Bowling Green State University

As noted in the introduction by Lee Nickoson and Mary P. Sheridan, *Writing Studies Research in Practice* blurs the distinction between methodologies and methods to encompass a variety of issues and trends in writing research. The collection's nineteen essays are divided into three parts, with part one exploring new approaches to composition research, part two examining research in the writing classroom, with particular focus on research centered on marginalized voices, and part three analyzing how knowledge is created through research. These essays explore a range of research contexts and settings, including programs and institutions, archives, community sites, and classrooms.

Themes of narrative and participant experience emerge early in the first section. The collection begins with Debra Journet's "Narrative Turns in Writing Studies Research," where the author examines the way that narrative influences research and creates disciplinary knowledge. Journet's main points are that narrative inflects a range of genres and that, while personal narrative is useful, as a field we need to develop criteria for determining when it is beneficial to scholarship. Liz Rohan's "Reseeing and Redoing: Making Historical Research at the Turn of the Millennium" also explores the value of the personal in one's research, particularly historical archival research. Rohan argues that choosing research subjects with whom we identify does not jeopardize a realistic representation of the research subject. Her claim is consistent with that of feminist researchers, who have long argued that personal attachments to a research subject do not necessarily impede a balanced representation and may in fact enhance the quality of the research.

Later essays in part one build upon issues of narrative in writing research to explore researcher and participant interaction. Cynthia L. Selfe and Gail E. Hawisher complicate the use of participants' personal narratives and experiences in "Exceeding the Bounds of the Interview," stating that devaluing participants' experiences in research leads to possible misinterpretation and a lack of interaction with participants. Selfe and Hawisher focus particularly on the interview, noting that a feminist approach to this method implies an interactive exchange between participant and researcher. Through their study of instant messaging, Christina Haas, Pamela Takayoshi, and Brandon Carr add to the idea of interaction in their discussion of the changing nature of composition. Symbols such as emoticons and other conventions common to text messaging, according to the authors' findings, shape not only interactions but also the making of knowledge.

Mary P. Sheridan provides a history of ethnographic research and describes the three stages of ethnography: preresearch and submitting to IRB boards, data collection, and triangulation. Sheridan points out that while these stages may seem tidy, they involve many negotiations amongst researcher, participant, and institutional systems. To assist in this negotiation, Sheridan calls for the inclusion of multiple voices to better understand the social factors at play. Issues in ethnography are also explored by A. Suresh Canagarajah in his piece "Autoethnography in the Study of Multilingual Writers," where he describes a method of self-study useful for analyzing language difference. The method, which entails observation of one's own writing practices, values the unique experience of transnational writing.

Passion and attachment to research are reoccurring themes throughout the collection and serve as a call to action for researchers. From a technofeminist perspective, Kristine L. Blair writes about personal attachments to research and its potential for social change. She emphasizes the need to put research into practice and cites her technology summer camp for preteen girls, Digital Mirror Computer Camp, as an example. This camp calls attention to the disparities in technology use amongst gender groups and offers positive change within the community. These passions and attachments shape not only the knowledge we produce but also the information we internalize, as Kristie Fleckenstein points out in her essay, "Reclaiming the Mind: Eco-Cognitive Research in Writing Studies." Fleckenstein uses an eco-cognitive model to discuss research and learning as a type of ecology, citing the online classroom as an example of how individuals process shared knowledge: "what becomes information is that which is important for the individual at that moment" (91). Knowledge is constructed through our own personal lenses; researchers should consider issues of cognition when designing research projects.

Part two is more directly focused on one's position as a researcher, with Lee Nickoson beginning the section with an examination of what constitutes teacher-research. The once-accepted definition of a teacher studying one's own classroom has broadened to include any educator conducting research to benefit the profession. The idea that research can directly benefit a community is also explored by Jeffrey T. Grabill in "Community-Based Research and the Importance of a Research Stance," which explores the idea of a research stance. Grabill notes that his own stance as a community-based researcher originates in his valuing the experiences of community member participants as well as the method's potential for social change.

Like Blair and Grabill, Asao B. Inoue calls attention to social issues in writing research, exploring race as a factor in writing assessment in his essay, "Racial Methodologies for Composition Studies." Since quantitative and qualitative studies have shown that students of color are more likely to receive lower writing assessment scores, Inoue calls for information on racial identity to be tracked along with assessment outcomes in order to more fairly design assessments and ensure validity and reliability. Similarly, Karen J. Lunsford calls for greater attention to international writing in composition research, pointing to the uniquely American first-year writing course compared to more specialized writing in international university settings.

Douglas Hesse explores writing research done at the program level, noting its varying purposes and audiences for both writing program administrators and graduate students. Steve Lamos adds to the conversation about program-level research in his essay "Institutional Critique in Composition Studies: Methodological and Ethical Considerations for Researchers." Lamos describes the value of digging for hidden gems in institutional research and the ethical concerns of whether to name human subjects when engaging in this type of study. Jenn Fishman builds upon these ideas as she discusses the importance of longitudinal program studies for the field, citing her experience with the valuable Stanford Study of Writing. The consensus in these essays is that program research offers benefits but also poses risks.

Part three begins with a debate about the role of quantitative versus qualitative research. Richard H. Haswell's "Quantitative Methods in Composition Studies" revisits the importance of quantitative research in composition studies. He cites the example of the WPA-L, where users regularly query the list for statistical data regarding first-year writing. Haswell points out that the information users are seeking often does not exist. He uses Mina Shaughnessy's suggestion of "diving in" to urge scholars to carefully attend to statistical analysis and also to analyze the research methods of others.

In close conversation with Haswell is Bob Broad's contribution, "Strategies and Passions in Empirical Research." Like many of the authors in this collection, Broad revisits the importance of acknowledging one's passions and attachments to research, including not only the research subject but also the research methods. Broad notes that research is messy and difficult to neatly define. He points out that, while Johanek begins her canonical book *Composing Research* with a call for unbiased research methods, such methods are nonexistent, and he points out that Johanek's personal attachments were her reason for writing the book.

Writing Studies also touches on the opportunities and challenges for Internet researchers. In their piece, "The Role of Activity Analysis in Writing Research," Mike Palmquist, Joan Mullin, and Glenn Blalock discuss three websites—WAC Clearinghouse, CompPile, and the Research Exchange Index or REx—to discuss the activity systems at play not only in the creation of these sites but also within composition studies. The Internet also provides new ethical concerns for researchers, as Heidi A. McKee and James E. Porter address in their chapter, "The Ethics of Conducting Writing Research on the Internet." The authors look at issues of public versus private writing and how resulting tensions affect ethical research practices. For example, when IRBs review a writing-related research project, a key factor in determining whether the project requires approval (and whether the writing being studied is private or public) is the level of interaction between researcher and participant. To better address the murky ethical issues of online data collection, the authors stress the need to be transparent about one's position as a researcher regardless of whether a project requires review.

Writing Studies Research and Practice does not detail the basic workings of surveys, interviews, and coding, but instead considers why it is we do the research that we do and why this question matters. Both novice and experienced writing researchers would find material to benefit their research practices in this collection. The book reveals emerging trends in the field while building on current conversations and traditions.

Bowling Green, Ohio

New Natures: Joining Environmental History with Science and Technology Studies, edited by Dolly Jørgensen, Finn Arne Jørgensen, and Sara B. Pritchard. Pittsburgh: University of Pittsburgh Press, 2013. 292 pp.

Reviewed by Danielle Hartke, University of Wisconsin-Milwaukee

Building on the emerging conversations of the past two decades, *New Natures* is a collection of essays that demonstrates the fruitfulness and transformative potential of interdisciplinary work between the fields of environmental history and science and technology studies (STS). Distinguished by its concern for fostering a theoretical dialogue, this collection explores how STS theory and concepts can both facilitate and extend the work of environmental history and yield wider insights about the power, values, and politics underlying our constructions of and relationships with nature. Though the introductory chapter acknowledges the mutual give-and-take between the two fields, *New Natures* specifically foregrounds the contributions of STS to environmental history. This emphasis reflects an overarching call for the more overt use of theory in the field of environmental history, in order to thicken or strengthen empirical studies and narratives as well as spur new developments and analysis.

Though the collection covers a variety of topics, including farming, trade, forestry, offshore drilling rigs, pollution, and outer space, Dolly Jørgensen, Finn Arne Jørgensen, and Sara B. Pritchard group the essays in *New Natures* into three often-overlapping sections. In STS fashion, all sections share an underlying concern for issues of power and the political. Part one consists of four essays that explore the construction and management of knowledge. In "The Natural History of Northeastern America: An Inexact Science," Anya Zilberstein, concerned with approaches for describing rapid environmental change, proposes that eighteenth-century American naturalists deliberately wrote vague historical and geographical accounts in order both to guard their work against obsolescence and accusations of incompetence and incompletion, as well as to encourage "ideas about the dynamism of nature," particularly for reasons of economic development (35). In "Farming and Not Knowing: Agnotology Meets Environmental History," Frank Uekotter states that ignorance, like knowledge, is constructed socially, as demonstrated by the production of ignorance in the development of German corn monoculture. In "Environmentalists on Both Sides: Enactments in the California Rigs-to-Reefs Debate," Dolly Jørgensen argues that it is the differing values and enactments of nature, not knowledge, at the root of the rigs-to-reef controversy. Interested in why some controversies close and others do not, Jørgensen's goal is to expose the two enactments in order to better understand how both parties can claim to be pro-environmental. In "The Backbone of Everyday Environmentalism: Cultural Scripting and Technological Systems," Finn Arne Jørgensen, through his analysis of Norwegian bottle recycling programs, argues that environmental action be embedded within effective sociotechnological systems, that consumers need to be enrolled, and that effective environmental action needs to be scripted.

The three essays of part two examine the construction of environmental expertise and its impact on environmental policy and human interaction with nature. In "The Soil Doctor: Hugh Hammond Bennett, Soil Conservation, and the Search for a Democratic Science," Kevin C. Armitage suggests that the environmental movement can utilize technological frames to remove expertise from its "ivory tower," placing it, instead, "outside, active, and created in conjunction with constituents" and making science a more public and democratic practice (89). In "Communicating Knowledge: The Swedish Mercury Group and Vernacular Science, 1965–1972," Michael Egan explores science's place in environmental politics. He states that reactive, uncertain science is "reduced" to part of a larger conversation in which it holds no special authority over other participatory groups (116). In "Signals in the Forest: Cultural Boundaries of Science in Bialowieza, Poland," Eunice Blavascunas argues for the importance of locals, especially their role in the creation, stabilization, and overturning of scientific facts: "If we want to learn something about the way science works, the answers will be found by looking not only at the labs and practices of scientists but at which facts are trusted by the people whose lives are affected" (130). Blavascunas questions what counts as science in environmental history when science practices are challenged, especially by non-scientists.

In the third part, consisting of five essays, the contributors directly engage with questions of networks, mobilities, and boundaries. In "The Production and Circulation of Standardized Karakul Sheep and Frontier Settlement in the Empires of Hitler, Mussolini, and Salazar," Tiago Saraiva offers a "transimperial narrative" that demonstrates the materialization of the expansionist ambitions of fascist governments (136). Saraiva moves past established disciplinary calls for the detailed examination of knowledge production by examining those laboratory processes in the context of social and economic spheres. In "Trading Spaces: Transferring Energy and Organizing Power in the 19th Century Atlantic Grain Trade," Thomas D. Finger argues for the importance of using both actor-network theory and systems thinking as analytical categories in order to more closely and fully analyze the relationships among sociotechnological arrangements and the scope and scale of environmental change. In "Situated Yet Mobile: Examining the Environmental History of Arctic Ecological Science," Stephen Bocking explores the tension between locality and circulation. Bocking uses Arctic research history to illustrate how science can be both situated and mobile, providing a way to understand the relationship among scientific practices, knowledge, and nature. In "White Mountain Apache Boundary-Work as an Instrument of Ecopolitical Liberation and Landscape Change," David Tomblin demonstrates how boundary-work can be reframed as a liberatory tool in order to understand "socially unjust distributions, applications, and consequences of science and technology" (181). His case study also provides an example of how local communities can resist, react, or adapt to the introduction of environmental technologies. In "NEOecology: The Solar System's Emerging Environmental History and Politics," Valerie A. Olson argues that near earth objects (NEOs) have become matters of concern, functioning as boundary objects, helping us to perceive outer space as connected to our Earthly environment and enabling environmental interpretations of cosmic history and human futures. More than just boundary objects, Olson is concerned with the political and social reasons for managing near/far Earth ecologies, as demonstrated in the language of the policies and petitions surrounding NEOs.

The collection closes with a positive look forward in Sverker Sörlin's epilogue, "Preservation in the Age of Enlightenment: STS and the History of Future Urban Nature." A renovation of both preservation and nature is happening, Sörlin argues, redefining and reviving them as entangled in the social. Nature's value, as shown in cities and other examples of cohabitation, is derived from this entanglement, rather than discounted because of it. With an emphasis on urban ecology, he conflates the old and tired boundaries between city and nature, suggesting new models and ways of thinking about nature, environmental policy, and humanity: "Nature should rather be seen as part of precisely that entanglement that becomes ever more characteristics of what it means to be human, which in turn means to be more and more part of the nonhuman" (223).

New Natures is a particularly valuable text for STS scholars and environmental historians as well as wider communities, including policy makers and other stakeholders. Within the field of rhetoric and composition, this collection of essays may also be useful and appropriate for rhetoricians of science and technology, environmental rhetoricians, and ecocompositionists. Though not directly related to teaching or the classroom, compositionists may also be interested in drawing parallels between the text's consideration of hierarchies of knowledge and expertise to their own work in composition theory and writing pedagogies. In so far as the essays cover a wide range of topics and STS theory, the book is perhaps not suitable as a primary text; however, its breadth is particularly useful for demonstrating the productivity of and potential avenues for interdisciplinary work, particularly between STS and environmental history, just as its title suggests. Contained within these covers are thirteen distinct and varied models of the deliberate application of theory from one field to empirical material in another, a move both valued in many fields and hailed by the editors as necessary for environmental historians. For academics and non-academics alike, the lucid prose, practical case studies and examples, and engaging style of the authors makes *New Natures* an insightful, pleasureable read.

Milwaukee, Wisconsin

Multimodal Literacies and Emerging Genres, edited by Tracey Bowen and Carl Whithaus. Pittsburgh: University of Pittsburgh Press, 2013. 356 pp.

Reviewed by Michael Madson, University of Minnesota–Twin Cities

As demands for technological literacy heighten, multimodality and genre have become some of the most fruitful—and fraught—concepts in composition studies. Seminal works by Gunther Kress, Anne Frances Wysocki, and the New London Group have helped teacher-scholars reconceptualize how composition is done, but much remains for both theory and practice. In terms of theory, technologies have opened new communicative possibilities, enabling and constraining new, hybridized genres that can challenge the literacy traditions of the academy. As a result, practical questions of how to implement theories of genre and multimodality, various as they are, can be tricky for students, teachers, and writing program administrators alike.

Multimodal Literacies and Emerging Genres, a collection edited by Tracey Bowen and Carl Whithaus, responds to this urgency, mapping how thirty composition teacher-scholars and students have responded to evolving literacies. To that end, part one (chapters one through five) emphasizes students' experiences, part two (chapters six through nine) turns to pedagogy, and part three (chapters ten through thirteen) discusses implications for writing programs. Although each of these chapters, in isolation, provides helpful insights, the book is especially useful when considered as a whole.

In the introduction, Bowen and Whithaus devote particular attention to genre, an arguably more contested site than multimodality. Specifically, they theorize genre in composition studies as falling between two poles. One views genre as relatively fixed and context invariant, as in Michael Halliday's systemic functional linguistics. The other, exemplified by Bakhtin's theories of semiotics, emphasizes generic fluidity and contextual variability. Except for perhaps Nathaniel Córdova, the book's contributors all stake genre in the rich middle ground between the two poles, which allows for a multiplicity of theoretical perspectives.

Within those perspectives, the contributors detail an impressive range of multimodal composition assignments, including ethnographies of various kinds, audio projects, PowerPoint presentations, constructions in virtual worlds, analyses of digital discourse communities, original paintings, posters, and T-shirts. This diversity in assignments, added to the book's diversity in theory, helps illuminate the benefits and challenges of multimodal, emerging genre pedagogies on several instructional levels. As a composition instructor, former student, and, briefly, program administrator, I thought this illumination across authorial voices was one of the book's most significant features. The book's internal referencing seems to encourage this kind of cross-chapter reading.

One possible benefit of teaching multimodality and emerging genres is student creativity and imagination. Erik Ellis, for instance, taught an assignment sequence in an upper-division writing course that leads to a multimedia essay. Like other composition assignments, especially those with a technological component, the multimedia essay requires careful scaffolding; so Ellis asked students to first complete the following exercises: a vivid description of a place, a summary and dramatic scene, a letter to a friend, and an account of evidence. These exercises guide students to develop a traditional essay in which they explore an original idea through an interesting viewpoint. Students then adapt their traditional essay for a DVD lasting no more than five minutes, creating the multimedia essay. One student, Katya, produced a DVD about her breakdancing passion, showing "a deeper, more visceral understanding of her experience and ideas" (58). Her essay is structured "so that it cleverly mirrors, in both image and sound, her cultural metamorphosis from a powerless and insecure insider for whom breakdancing was initially 'beautiful, intimidating, and extremely foreign' to a conflicted yet confident insider" (59–60). Another student, Merced, designed strategic blackouts, camera close-ups, and an emotional voiceover in his multimedia essay about walking for hours during a West Point training session. The multimodal assignment, Ellis notes, had allowed students to exercise their creativity and imagination while, at the same time, deepening their rhetorical savvy and increasing the relevance of the writing course.

Book contributors besides Ellis report similar benefits. Collectively, they argue that multimodal assignments can enhance student abilities to argue visually, synthesize multiple positions, and use information ethically; compose for diverse, even global audiences; peer review and revise; and collaborate across national borders. For teacher-scholars and writing program administrators, multimodality and emerging genres can foster a reimagining of the rhetorical canons, partially fulfill the disciplinary obligation to accurately describe human communication, and maintain the applicability of composition curricula.

Since multimodality and emerging genres typically involve communication technologies, such assignments require some degree of technical know-how. Students and instructors, consequently, may face anxiety, doubts, and other frustrations as they learn new devices, plug-ins, platforms, and productions. In fact, during a focus group discussing a multimodal assignment they completed in the virtual world *Second Life*, students were asked to write their reactions on notecards. Among those reactions were "HELP," "Grrr," "HELL,""BLEH," "Anger," "NIGHTMARE," "stress," and "HOW DO I DO IT??" (130). Likewise, fifty-three percent of the students reported not "really" enjoying the *Second*

Life assignment, owing, perhaps, to the steep learning curve and maintenance problems (129–30). The contributors show that even if students do enjoy a multimodal assignment, they might question its value, struggle to transfer the skills they acquired, or avoid creative risks, especially in introductory courses.

Complicating matters further, composition assignments that involve multimodality and emerging genres can be challenging to evaluate or lack institutional capital. Institutional capital is key for developing multimodal writing programs, which must prepare and support instructors, develop curricula, secure administrative resources, and conduct regular, program-wide assessments. Chapter twelve describes these considerable tasks in depth, discussing how the composition program at Miami University instituted classroom, curricular, and programmatic changes, resulting in the ongoing Digital Writing Collaborative. Chapter thirteen offers another programmatic perspective, describing the efforts of St. Lawrence University faculty members to update rhetorical pedagogies there, culminating in the Rhetoric and Communication Institute for faculty development. Both chapters illustrate the necessity of adequate funding and administrative support, as well as "a critical conceptual shift regarding teaching and learning" (324). None of these tasks are easily accomplished, and writing program administrators seeking to establish multimodal, emerging genre pedagogies can potentially glean much from the detailed experiences of St. Lawrence and Miami.

Such benefits and challenges, cutting across chapters, illustrate the variety, candor, and high relief of *Multiliteracies and Emerging Genres*, which helpfully blends theory with practice on multiple levels. For these reasons alone, the book makes an important contribution to composition studies. Of course, the editors did not intend to be comprehensive, and readers might be left with numerous questions that merit additional inquiry. One question might be the responsibility of composition instructors in teaching technological literacies. In the introduction, Bowen and Whithaus claim that "[o]ur job is neither to lead [students] into this changing world of multimodality nor to hold them back from it" (5), suggesting that teacher-scholars can occupy a position of neutrality. The succeeding chapters, however, do not always support this claim, even implying that such neutrality is impossible. Thus, the book is best read as an open-ended dialogue, not as a single, cohesive treatise.

A second question might be how multimodality and emerging genres have been theorized and applied in graduate courses, courses outside the U.S., and other second-language composition courses. Chapter seven does hint in these directions, explaining a collaboration between a Swedish PhD course entitled "Fiction for Engineers," a U.S. master's course in Victorian poetry, and a U.S. sophomore survey course of American literature. Yet, given the expanding interest in translingual writing, the needs of composition students from diverse heritages, and the cultural values embedded in communications technologies, a wider range of composition courses might have strengthened the book. So, too, might have more sustained discussions of surveillance, privacy, access, mediation, agency, and other pressing issues that attend the uses of digital technologies. These, however, might fall beyond the book's scope, and despite its few shortcomings, I think Bowen and Whithaus have created an approachable, well-conceived resource on some of the most generative concepts in composition studies.

Minneapolis, Minnesota

Experimental Writing in Composition: Aesthetics and Pedagogies, by Patricia Suzanne Sullivan. Pittsburgh, PA: University of Pittsburgh Press, 2012. 188 pp.

Reviewed by Dan Martin, University of Central Florida

Patricia Sullivan's *Experimental Writing in Composition* dissects the intersections between aesthetics, experimental writing, dialectics, and composition pedagogy. Examining a range of pedagogical texts and arguments for using alternative forms in composition like "mixed genres, fragmented texts, collages, experiments in grammar, and multimodal forms"(1), *Experimental Writing* teases out, analyzes, and comments on how theories of aesthetics (with a specific focus on the avant-garde) impact composition pedagogy. Special consideration is given to the avant-garde and its relationship to experimental writing because of the similarities between the arguments avant-gardists use to validate their work as an art form and the arguments composition scholars use to validate alternative writing as an art form. In this text Sullivan digs deep into alternative writing theory and pedagogy, providing a thorough examination of how aesthetics and dialectics have shaped experimental discourses and how dialectics have impacted the development and application of composition pedagogy within specific social and historical contexts. Her definition of dialectics is rooted in dissoi logoi, a concept from classical rhetoric where one side of an argument attempts to establish itself as the dominant side while arguing against the opposing side. Sullivan argues that dialectics contain tensions that seep into aesthetic theories and composition pedagogies, forcing the reshaping of both.

    The first section of Sullivan's text comprehensively historicizes experimental writing pedagogy and theory in composition. The second section examines the collage form as a potential balance between academic writing (argument papers, research proposals, and rhetorical analysis essays) and experimental writing. Beneath Sullivan's analyses and comparisons of pedagogies, aesthetics, dialectics, and experimental discourses are fragments of broader and familiar questions about teaching composition: Should composition teach academic forms, or allow students to explore experimental forms? Should, or can there be a balance between academic discourse and alternative writing? Does the experimental have to disrupt the traditional? Sullivan suggests that teachers and students work to develop and adopt pedagogies for teaching and evaluating experimental writing—an idea reiterated throughout *Experimental Writing*—but she "does not argue for teaching experimental writing in composition classrooms; nor do I explain how to teach such texts" (2). I wanted to review this book because I needed a resource to combat my own struggles moving between traditional and experimental forms. Balancing the use of academic and experimental forms in the classroom is difficult because, as Sullivan argues, truly experimental writing requires composition teachers and students to take risks in the classroom if they want to build better composition pedagogy.

Chapter one examines competing expressivist arguments for using alternative writing pedagogy from Winston Weathers to Peter Elbow. Sullivan begins this chapter with a lengthy explication of Weathers' *Alternative Rhetoric* where we learn that experimental writing is heavily grounded in expressivism—a composition theory that sees all individuals as artists and catalysts for liberating themselves from institutional usurpation. Expressivist concerns for using experimental writing in composition contain similar dialectical concerns echoed by avant-garde artists. For example, students trying to achieve expressive freedom through the use of experimental forms in art or writing often struggle with an intense desire to gain individual autonomy while yearning to be part of the larger social collective. This leads Sullivan to contend that examining aesthetics like the avant-garde may help combat similar dialectical struggles in composition. Sullivan argues that the "histories, theories, and critiques of avant-garde art [and other aesthetics] can help composition and aesthetic scholars think through dialectics of the individual and the institution" (17–18). Her unique methodology for using aesthetics as a lens to examine alternative composition theory opens up new possibilities for aesthetic scholars to engage composition work and to gain insight into how aesthetics can serve as a catalyst for overcoming dialectical conflicts within composition. Aesthetics like the avant-garde provide a blue print for how to validate art in culture and how to disrupt traditional notions of art. Composition scholars can use this blueprint (histories, theories, and critiques) of aesthetics to think about how to use and validate experimental writing in composition. Therefore the arguments and approaches that aesthetic scholars and artists have used to address dialectical concerns may be of value to composition scholars.

Chapter two analyzes views of alternative discourses from Geoffrey Sirc to Terry Myers Zawacki, and scrutinizes limitations in arguments that politicize experimental writing. This chapter outlines how avant-garde artists have defined their work historically, exposing the deep-seeded roots of avant-garde theory and its indirect connectivity to experimental writing. This chapter also identifies a variety of expressivist arguments for using experimental writing in composition. Sullivan ends this chapter advocating that teachers should be more introspective of how they blend alternative writing theory into composition assignments, evaluating standards, and pedagogies. In chapter three, "The Crisis of Judgment in Composition: Evaluating Experimental Student Writing," Sullivan examines methods and arguments for how to evaluate alternative writing more closely. Her main concern in this chapter is how to situate experimental writing within firmly established, long-standing, institutional evaluation standards for traditional writing. This chapter examines several arguments for how to evaluate experimental writing from Elizabeth Rankin to Ronald A. DePeter. Abandoning traditional criteria to grade alternative writing can be perilous for teachers; giving up their credibility to make evaluative judgments can leave teachers without the authority necessary to provide adequate and useful feedback on student work. Sullivan terms this experience "evaluative paralysis" and suggests using Lyotard's theory of "marrying…prudence and imagination" to argue that teachers can use their experiences, education, and intuition to invent new criteria to evaluate experimental writing that is highly reflective of student discourse, opinions, and input (98). This leads Sullivan to claim that arguments for how to evaluate experimental writing in composition are both a response to the difficulties teachers have evaluating experimental writing and a creator of a problematic situation (or "crisis") in composition that begins when teachers abandon their evaluation standards, limiting their authority in the classroom.

Chapter four, "Collage: Pedagogies, Aesthetics, and Reading Students' Texts," analyzes the aesthetics within pedagogies for teaching collage and highlights several different arguments for teaching collage in composition from Tristan Tzara's to Betsy Nies, noting that some pedagogical approaches to collage are more disruptive to academic forms than other approaches. Composition teachers will appreciate the extensive analysis and historical overview of collage theory and collage pedagogy in this chapter, and they will find several examples of collage pedagogy, collage forms, and standards for evaluating collage. Sullivan applies concepts for evaluating alternative writing from chapter three to the evaluation of her own students' collages. Readers may infer after reading this chapter that collage provides the best opportunity to bridge aesthetics, art, and writing together, but Sullivan is not completely convinced that collage is capable of providing a balanced and critical lens for commenting on social and political concerns because most collage pedagogies place extremely different values on the use and evaluation of collage in composition. However, Sullivan proclaims that a student collage text "cracks open my pedagogy and puts my criteria for evaluating their writing on the table for discussion" (146). "It is this pedagogical use of the collage," she notes, "which I see as one of the most valuable uses of experimental writing in the classroom" (130). Collage pedagogies provide a space for students and teachers to work through creating and evaluating experimental writing together.

Chapter five is a postscript on multimodal composition where we learn that arguments for teaching multimodal and collage forms have failed to escape the same "dialectical tensions of avant-garde aesthetics and contemporary composition pedagogies" (147). In this very brief chapter, Sullivan continues to examine how composition addresses dialectical tensions within three popular texts for teaching multimodal compositions: Cynthia Selfe's *Multimodal Composition: Resources for Teachers*, Jeff Rice's *The Rhetoric of Cool*, and Anne Wysocki's *Writing New Media*. These texts argue for the value of multimodal forms in composition; however, Rice, Selfe, and Wysocki represent different extremes in this argument. Selfe invites the use of academic literacies and multimodal forms even though she argues against the superiority of print literacies, while scholars like Rice argue against the use of academic literacies with multimodal forms. Ultimately this chapter, like the entire book, argues that we cannot separate composition pedagogy from the technologic and aesthetic principles that are bound to mass culture. Sullivan does not claim that aesthetics like the avant-garde are directly responsible for experimental writing in composition; nor does she argue that there is a direct correlation between the two. She also stops shy of claiming that we can learn something valuable for composition from aesthetics, but she never wavers from her main argument in this text that the teaching of composition should focus on experimental writing just as much as academic writing. Perhaps the most useful aspect of this text is the critical space it provides for composition teachers and scholars to think about experimental and traditional writing together.

Orlando, Florida

Thomas De Quincey: British Rhetoric's Romantic Turn, by Lois Peters Agnew. Carbondale and Edwardsville: SIUP, 2012. 165 pp.

Reviewed by Patricia Mellon Moore, Colorado State University–Pueblo

Lois Peter Agnew's well-researched and comprehensive study, *Thomas De Quincey: British Rhetoric's Romantic Turn*, is one in a series produced by SUNY on Rhetoric in the Modern Era, edited by Arthur E. Walzer and Edward Schiappa. The series is intended for "nonspecialists—graduate students coming to the study of a theorist for the first time and professors broadly interested in the rhetorical tradition" (Foreword).

While noting that most histories of British rhetoric end with Richard Whately's 1828 *Elements of Rhetoric*, often considered the final word on the subject, Agnew claims in her introduction that, because their ideas are non-traditional, the works of lesser known nineteenth century British theorists are equally important to rhetorical history. They point out the expanding parameters used to define rhetoric and bring it into the modern era when technology and culture were changed by the industrial revolution. Although Thomas De Quincey is best known for his autobiographical work concerning the use of opium, his oeuvre also includes many essays on rhetoric, language, and style. It is through these works, Agnew argues, that De Quincey has become particularly important among the often overlooked nineteenth century theorists. His "radically distinct" perspective on language and public life, although grounded in Aristotle, reflects the cultural circumstances of the nineteenth century and "fills in the gaps" left by most accounts of rhetorical history (1).

In chapter two, "De Quincey's Life," Agnew describes the sociocultural and educational experiences that shaped not only De Quincey's life but also his "complex interpretation" of those experiences resulting in his somewhat unconventional theory of rhetoric (18). Key elements in De Quincey's life include the death of his father and of his two sisters early in his life, a complicated relationship with his mother, and an unstable educational path, which he chose to abandon before his final exams at Oxford. In addition, financial difficulties that began with the death of his father grew exponentially throughout his life and were never completely resolved until his daughters took command of his finances. Significant influences in De Quincey's life include Romantic writers Wordsworth, Coleridge, and Pope, with whom he did not always agree, but who helped shape the Romantic impulse that eventually manifested in his theories of language and in his writing. Another strong influence, Agnew points out, was opium, which De Quincy used with little restraint at various times throughout his life. The events of and influences on De Quincey's life, coupled with his "eccentricity and sociability, genius and ineptitude, obsession with organization and affinity for chaos" were integral parts of his formation of a "dialogic rhetorical theory that is simultaneously grounded in tradition and radically subversive" (41). De Quincey came to believe that every subject, whether in writing or in life, is diverse and multidimensional with a latent number of valid " alternate possibilities" which he consistently explored, largely through his own writing (18–44).

In chapter three, "Eddying Thoughts and Dialogical Potential," Agnew summarizes the five essays through which De Quincey develops the major principles of his rhetoric. These essays, each discussing one of De Quincey's key themes are "Rhetoric," "Style," "Language," "Conversation," and "A Brief Appraisal of Greek Literature in Its Foremost Pretensions," were published in a "periodical dedicated to intellectual matters" (47). While De Quincey despised the periodical format and considered himself a "hack in an endless struggle with deadlines" (Devlin, qtd. in Agnew 46), the magazine work, with its unyielding deadlines and timely paychecks, ultimately formed De Quincey as a writer.

Agnew claims that much of De Quincey's own writing about rhetoric seems abstract, but she works through that obscurity to clearly explain and define the unique perspectives involved in his particular rhetoric as she delves into De Quincey's criticisms of John Donne, Francis Bacon, and Sir Walter Raleigh, among others. Agnew describes and clarifies De Quincey's distinct line between rhetoric and eloquence, claiming that rhetoric has much more to do with the written text than with oratory, yet still establishing a clear connection between rhetoric and conversation. De Quincy blurs a very traditional boundary but still manages to revitalize a rhetoric seemingly lost in the nineteenth century's language of business and industry

In chapter four, "De Quincey's 'Science of Style,'" Agnew continues her discussion of De Quincey's essays, calling attention to his perception that the intellectual energy of the Romantic era was fizzling out with the onset of mass marketed publications. "For De Quincey," she explains, "the art of style facilitates the connections and modifications that are integral to the development of complex ideas" (83). As with rhetoric, De Quincey saw the nineteenth century as lacking in effective writing and clear thinking which was due, ironically, to the inferior quality of printed material available, such as the magazine through which he published his own work. Particularly interesting in this chapter, in this age of equality and feminism, is Agnew's discussion concerning De Quincey's opinion of French style, as well as his opinion of "well educated women not professionally given to literature," who "might offer hope for the British language" through their communication style (100). Here Agnew calls attention to De Quincey's complicated relationship with women as well as his gender specific conclusions that, while not quite contemporary, acknowledges repression of women in industrial society (101).

Having devoted a large part of the book thus far to De Quincy's rather unconventional theories of rhetoric, in chapter five, "De Quincey's Writing: Dialogic Rhetoric in Action," Agnew goes on to demonstrate, through careful readings of selected passages, how the major principles of his non-traditional rhetoric apply to De Quincey's own work. Disagreeing with Frederick W. Haberman, who claims that De Quincey's rhetorical theory is egocentric, Agnew argues that while De Quincey did not "intend to reserve his theory for himself" (104), it is still challenging to find the precise principles that do guide his writing, which she sees as an "intricately woven pattern that juxtaposes personal reflection, cultural and historical background, encounters with other people, and investigation of varying approaches to a subject..." (105). Difficult though it may be, Agnew does an excellent job of indicating where and how De Quincey's work adheres to the principles of rhetoric he has set forth in his essays. The passages she has chosen are lively and engaging, and show the full range of De Quincey's interests while illuminating his particular rhetoric, style, and language.

Chapter six, "De Quincey's Place in Rhetorical Histories," places De Quincey into nineteenth century Britain, an era in which traditional western rhetoric had begun to lose its purpose in an industrialized society. De Quincey's theories, which were radically multidimensional, infinitely subjective, and rife with "alternatives" and "possibilities," disrupted established assumptions surrounding traditional western rhetoric, and, according to Agnew, De Quincey was not only the creator of the change that was about to occur, but he ushered it in. He was the bridge upon which later theorists and writers would cross from the early nineteenth century to the latter part. De Quincey's "possibilities," "dimensions," and "alternatives" would be their destination.

Opinions vary on the actual value of De Quincey's work and on his place in the history of rhetoric. Later in chapter six, after considering the matter thoroughly, Agnew claims that De Quincey deserves attention if only because his "theory is startling in its rejection of the civic mission that many of his contemporaries had assumed to be rhetoric's primary domain" (PG). Rhetoric, like so many other aspects of a civilized lifestyle, has survived only because its theories are adaptable to cultural change.

In this volume, Agnew presents an extensive discussion of Thomas De Quincey, a little known British literary figure, whose ideas and theories of rhetoric, conversation, and style are overlooked in the history of rhetoric. She guides the reader through the cultural changes inherent to the nineteenth century and places De Quincey into a proper place within that history. After perusing this book, a reader understands the philosophical development of this

British intellectual and why he should be considered important to students of rhetoric, the Romantic era, and the Enlightenment era. Although condensed into a mere 165 pages, Agnew's extensive research is of value to students of rhetoric, particularly those encountering De Quincey for the first time.

The goal of the SUNY series, Rhetoric in the Modern Era, is "to prompt and sponsor book-length treatments of important rhetorical theorists and of philosophers and literary theorists who make substantial contributions to our understanding of language and rhetoric" (Foreword). Agnew's highly accessible book certainly meets and even exceeds that goal, and the quality of this book definitely invites readers to seek out companion volumes in the SUNY series.

Pueblo, Colorado

The Online Writing Conference: A Guide for Teachers and Tutors, by Beth L. Hewett. Portsmouth, NH: Boynton/Cook, 2010. 184 pp.

Reviewed by Sushil K. Oswal, University of Washington

Beth L. Hewett's *The Online Writing Conference* addresses three under-represented yet significant areas of online writing instruction (OWI): the theory and practice of textual exchanges, the nature and substance of dialogic interactions, and the wisdom of depending on traditional face-to-face writing theories and pedagogies to drive the work of OWI. She pays close attention to tutoring approaches based on textual interactions with online learners, an often overlooked field of inquiry. The added relevance of these textual approaches is becoming obvious from the perspective of disability and accessibility in light of the emerging research in OWI.

Hewett questions the privileging of oral discourse (through telephone and audio-visual conversations) in online tutoring, and argues for reinstating the student-generated text as central to the teacher/tutor/student conference. In her own words, "OWI necessarily requires the teacher/tutor to use one-to-one computer-based teaching strategies: to teach deliberately and to intervene through online conferences using the student's text, instructional commentary, and other sources" (xvi). Hewett rightly questions the relevance of summative remarks in audio-visual interactions in lieu of textual ones.

Hewett's focus on the dialogical interactions between instructor and student in both synchronic and asynchronic encounters also serves a useful pedagogical purpose. Whereas the research on all kinds of online interactions among student-peers abounds, efforts for understanding one-to-one online student-instructor exchanges in OWI so far have been relegated to sporadic discussions in textbook chapters and journal articles. Hewett surmises that "the silence [about instructor-based one-to-one online instruction] suggests that one-to-one teaching does not occur online, that one-to-one online pedagogy is transparent, or that one-to-one interactions are not considered teaching at all" (xvi). Here, the author reminds us that writing center pedagogy is ultimately a one-to-one proposition between teacher/tutor and student and that this arrangement is as relevant in online tutoring contexts as it is in face-to-face contexts. To fill this lacuna in the OWI literature, Hewett articulates a theoretical framework for "problem-based teaching" accompanied by a wide range of practical strategies for one-to-one settings.

Another area where Hewett provides a useful critique of the current OWI is in her questioning of the transference of face-to-face theory to online settings. She stresses the need for exploring the full potential of the virtual pedagogical setting so that OWI develops its own medium-specific theory. She explains that traditional writing pedagogy is different from OWI in that student composing and instructor feedback in the former go through a type of textual and face-to-face, interpersonal and interactional cycle, whereas the interactions in OWI are intrinsically textual. She asserts that "the fundamentally textual nature of teaching and learning in the virtual environment is at odds with such a one-to-one transference" (xvii). Hewett backs up her claims with the growing OWI research literature. She claims that this research shows that the convergence of traditional writing instruction theory and related pedagogical practices in online settings brings some disconnects between contemporary composition theory and practice to the forefront, which Hewett labels as a lack of "semantic integrity." She sees this disconnect not as a flaw but an opportunity: for OWI to develop writing instruction theory specific to online settings and subsequently distinguish itself from traditional instructional theory. Her hope is that this new OWI theory, with its "semantic integrity," will assist students in learning what they need to know to develop and improve their writing on a case-by-case basis from a problem-centered perspective.

Hewett further suggests that at this stage in OWI's development as a field the theories guiding our practice must be drawn from observations of and speculations about how students write in online environments. "The result of semantic integrity," according to Hewett, "is instructional language that provides sufficient information to students, offers clear guidance about potential next steps (which includes teaching students how to make choices and encouraging them to do so), and works to prompt new or different thinking—all through textual commentary" (xviii). She stresses that "[t]o teach through text—which includes but goes beyond holding online discussions, lecturing by means of digital handouts, or providing summative evaluation of writing—is a challenging task" (xviii). Questioning prevalent theories of composing—expressivist, social constructionist, and postprocess—all of which exhort teachers against direct intervention in students' composing processes and allot a greater role to in-class peer interaction and feedback, Hewett explains that in online pedagogy "what is digitally recorded is the sum total of the interaction. Without the sounds of phatic language and the unspoken messages of body and facial language, digital intervention is the only way to teach writing and revising" (xix). Hewett acknowledges that some of the intervention strategies she proposes here are implicit in the eclectic practices of contemporary face-to-face writing instruction. Later in the book, she expands on three such eclectic practices: modeling writing and revision, consistently using targeted mini-lessons that require student action, and listing next steps that explicitly guide students toward future drafts.

Besides exploring these three central themes, the book is also rich in ongoing commentary on the availability of training for instructors, the missing disciplinary standards for quality control of online writing courses mushrooming all over the country, and much-needed best-practices documents to guide the online classroom.

If I were to point out some of the areas where this book could go further in the next edition to meet our writing centers' burning needs today, tutoring for multimodal writing and specialized audiences would be on the top of my list. While Hewett's focus on text and text-based feedback is well reasoned, this discussion could also provide us a better understanding of the multimodal trends in composing she outlines elsewhere. As Hewett mentions, many of us are employing sound and video to connect with our students remotely whether or not they are enrolled in our online writing courses. Online conferencing research is already contributing to this aspect of face-to-face learning (see Ascuena and Kiernan) but more research and theory is needed. Likewise, the burgeoning population of English language learners in our courses and the entry of students with disabilities in large numbers into our colleges during the past decade also beg for sophisticated approaches in order to serve these groups sufficiently. Recent scholarship from the perspective of disability studies has begun to address some of these issues but we must also deal with these concerns inclusively in all other research (e.g., Babcock; Brizee, Sousa, and Driscoll; Hewett; Keidaisch and Dinitz). A multimodal approach is an option worth exploring to meet these learners' specific needs. I'm sure that Hewett is cognizant of these concerns as she speaks more broadly of some of these gaps (xv).

From this reviewer's perspective, between these two pedagogical poles (face-to-face and online/multimodal) lies the blended, or the hybrid—the space where face-to-face and online meet, mingle, intersect, and interact. Many of the questions about OWI raised in this book and elsewhere might be answered if we examine those transitional zones between the two pedagogies where the characteristics of the two appear in one shared space, sometimes blending into a single whole, becoming one, and at other times, standing apart. The phenomenon observed on these borderlines might pinpoint the causes of why the teaching and learning members of the face-to-face and online communities act and react in certain ways. They might underscore the performance factors that stand behind the failure or success in each of these environments.

As early as 1984 Stephen North wrote, "Our job is to produce better writers, not better writing" (76). Hewett's *The Online Writing Conference* does a marvelous job of enriching our repertoire of techniques and strategies for interacting with our nascent writers in virtual settings.

Tacoma, Washington

Works Cited

Ascuena, Andrea, and Julia Kiernan. "The Problem of Email: Working to Decentralize Consultant Authority in Online Writing Centers." *Praxis: A Writing Center Journal* 5.2 (2008): Web. 11 Nov. 2011.

Babcock, Rebecca. *Tell Me How It Reads: Tutoring Deaf and Hearing Students in the Writing Center*. Washington: Gallaudet UP, 2012. Print.

Brizee, Allen, Morgan Sousa, and Dana Lynn Driscoll. "Writing Centers and Students with Disabilities: The User-Centered Approach, Participatory Design, and Empirical Research as Collaborative Methodologies." *Computers and Composition* 29.4 (2012): 341–66. Print.

Hewett, Beth L. "Helping Students with Learning Disabilities: Collaboration between Writing Centers and Special Services." *The Writing Lab Newsletter* 25.3 (2000): 1–5. Print.

Keidaisch, J., and Sue Dinitz. "Changing Notions of Difference in the Writing Center: The Possibilities of Universal Design." *Writing Center Journal* 27.2 (2007): 39–59. Print.

North, Stephen M. "The Idea of a Writing Center." *College English* 46.5 (1984): 433–46. Print.

A Synthesis of Qualitative Studies of Writing Center Tutoring 1983–2006, by Rebecca Day Babcock, Kellye Manning, Travis Rogers, and Courtney Goff. New York: Peter Lang Publishing, 2012. 137 pp.

Reviewed by Martha Wilson Schaffer, Bowling Green State University

A Synthesis of Qualitative Studies of Writing Center Tutoring 1983–2006 is a meta-research project that first gathers and describes the findings of multiple qualitative studies of what transpires during writing center tutorials and then attempts to develop a theory to inform and enhance writing tutorial practices. The text begins with a brief overview of the development of writing centers, and a discussion of the common issues faced by writing centers, such as how tutors collaborate and how tutees respond to directive and non-directive tutoring. The authors' self-described impetus for the project is the need for "a theory grounded in data rather than in abstractions in order to present a complete model of what actually happens in tutoring sessions" (4). Organizing the reviewed studies according to various factors that impact what occurs during tutoring sessions as well as what results from the tutoring session, Babcock et al. focus on findings rather than researchers' judgments and opinions in order to cleanly present the data. After detailing five factors and findings about each, the authors offer their own conclusions, including a description of what occurs in any tutoring session. Ultimately, though, data synthesis leads the authors to argue that writing centers should reconsider notions of collaboration, success, and direct versus indirect tutoring to find a middle ground where tutoring techniques blend "the ways of the old grammarians and the techniques of writing teachers who want their students to focus on self-expression" (123).

In their introduction, the authors describe the impetus for the project as well as their research methods, arguing that now is the time for a theory of writing centers built from the collected findings of qualitative studies and focused on what transpires during a writing tutorial. Chapters two through eight detail findings from the qualitative studies that the research team reviewed. Chapter two catalogues personal characteristics that impact the tutorial, largely in terms of "credibility, attractiveness, and power of the interlocutor" (13). These characteristics of interlocutors include knowledge, experience, race, sex, age, native language, (dis)ability, cultural identity, preparation, positive or negative attitude, writing skills, and appearance. Chapters two through eight all conclude with a summary of bulleted findings about each of these factors.

Chapter three describes external influences on the writing tutorial, beginning with "[t]he entire discourse community as a whole, and Standard English in particular" (27). From there, the authors describe findings regarding the impact of the university, academic discourse, the subject, the course, the teacher, the director, other people, duration of the tutoring relationship, expectations, cultural milieu, physical space, time of session(s), and medium (face to face and/or online). Chapter four recounts findings that explore communication—the tools by which the tutor and tutee relate to one another interpersonally through the tutoring relationship. Listening, questioning, praise, negotiation, laughter, connectedness—these are the discourse features and non-verbal cues that comprise the categories in this chapter. Though the authors work to avoid making sweeping conclusions in the chapters, they do acknowledge some common findings. The discussion of praise, for example, reveals that some researchers found that praise was sometimes misinterpreted—tutors used it as politeness, rather than as genuine commentary on the effectiveness of a written text, or of writing practices; tutees assumed the praise was genuine and became upset when the tutor then questioned the practice or paper later. Though this finding alone doesn't lead to any specific prescription for how and when to employ praise in communicating during a writing tutorial, it does offer opportunity for readers to consider how, why, and with what possible effects the participants in a tutoring session relate interpersonally.

In chapter five, the authors explore the nature of roles in the tutoring session, demonstrating that each person plays various roles in the writing tutorial that are "mostly consciously chosen" (59). Some of the role categories described here include (non)directive, (non)confrontational, controlling, (non)authoritarian, gendered, and resistant. The discussion of the various roles that tutors and tutees assume during tutoring sessions demonstrates a rift between what tutors are taught to do and what they actually do, as well as a rift between what produces successful results for tutees, both materially (an improved paper) and affectively (satisfaction with the tutoring and confidence in developing writing skills). The authors offer a rather short discussion of emotion in chapter six, where tutor and tutee experiences are categorized rather simplistically in terms of frustration, fear, guilt, confusion, and comfort. Chapter seven details findings pertaining to temperament. Again rather simplistically, the categorization identifies three temperaments: (in)sensitivity, confidence, and empathy. Here the authors generate some conclusive observations based on the studies they have reviewed. For example, Babcock et al. argue that "[t]he natural disposition for most tutors is to empathize with a tutee to establish rapport" (84).

The authors discuss outcomes of tutoring sessions in chapter eight, arguing that all of the previously discussed factors converge to create the "focus" of the writing tutorial, which "results in the outcome" (87). Though they recognize at the outset that outcomes can be affective, cognitive, and/or material, the writers do not sort the findings according to these categories, but rather organize findings by session focus, authority, material outcomes, and relationship status. As to the last of these, Babcock, Manning, and Rogers argue that relationship status is "characterized by solidarity, trust and comfort (or lack thereof), and is displayed in the tutoring session through collaboration and conflict, authority, and empowerment" (91).

The concluding chapter provides a helpful exploration of the difficulty in drawing general conclusions about their collected findings as a result of differing terminology around the notion of success. Rather than simply serving as an explanation for their inability to offer something akin to "guidelines for good writing tutorials," this explanation anchors the main argument of the text: writing centers, tutors, and teachers need to rethink how success is defined in the context of tutoring sessions. The authors also invoke Marysia Johnson's "theory of coconstruction" in secondary language acquisition studies and Lev Vygotsky's "scaffolding" in order to offer an additional challenge to the notion of collaboration in tutorial situations. With these concepts, the authors argue that tutoring is a negotiation of the participants, in which both have personalities, communication styles, expectations, and desires for results that affect the session, either to its detriment or success. In closing, Babcock, Manning, and Rogers find that what theoretically should occur in tutoring (non-directive, student-centered approaches) is not what practically happens in writing tutorials (directive, text-centered or tutor-centered approaches). This may very well be an indication that familiar concepts for judging a session successful are not in practice for tutors or for tutees. The prescription is for more research into a "middle ground," where effective writing center practices are a combination of "complementary features from the ways of the old grammarians and the techniques of writing teachers who want their students to focus on self-expression" (123).

A Synthesis of Qualitative Studies of Writing Center Tutoring 1983–2006 offers teachers, tutors, and writing center administrators a wealth of findings from various qualitative studies about what happens during writing center tutorials. Findings are categorized and discussed in a clear, direct, and largely unadulterated fashion. Though the collected findings are probably too basic for experienced writing center scholars, the text would serve nicely as a quick reference to a great deal of information. And beyond writing center walls, this text would be an excellent resource for writing teachers with only a peripheral, and largely lore-inspired notion of what happens in writing tutorials. Babcock et al. note at the outset of the book that distrust and misunderstandings between writing center tutors and teachers continue to make the work difficult, and their work goes a long way to both demonstrate that much goes on during writing center tutorials (it is complex), and that tutors are conscious of and attendant to the myriad complications. Babcock, Manning, Rogers, and Goff also nicely set the stage for further research, not just in the call for further development of effective writing center practices, but even within the descriptions of studies in chapters two through eight, where an absence of collected qualitative work on a variety of tutoring factors and issues is evident. Though the conclusions fall short of offering writing center theory, as promised in their introduction, the authors effectively explain how theories and prescriptions might be premature—that basic notions of success, collaboration, and directive tutoring practices need further consideration.

Bowling Green, Ohio

Evolutionary Rhetoric: Sex, Science, and Free Love in Nineteenth-Century Feminism, by Wendy Hayden. Carbondale: Southern Illinois UP, 2013. 259 pp.

Reviewed by Jacqueline Schiappa, University of Minnesota–Twin Cities

In *Evolutionary Rhetoric: Sex, Science, and Free Love in Nineteenth-Century Feminism*, author Wendy Hayden successfully recovers unfamiliar nineteenth-century women's free-love rhetoric and history. To these women, free-love represented the freedom to choose monogamy without marriage, to marry without forgoing legal autonomy, increased female agency in reproductive, health and labor rights, and to access information regarding female sexual health. Her investigation reveals several interesting rhetorical applications of scientific discourse by free-love feminists from the late 1800s to 1907 in their efforts to reject the state-sanctioned institution of marriage. Extending the scholarship of free-love researchers John C. Spurlock, Hal D. Sears, and Joanne E. Passet, Hayden's attention to feminist discourse meets her hope to "enlarge our view of nineteenth-century women's rhetorical practices" (23). The author's examination of the free-love movement centers on the rhetoric of eight key rhetors and the emerging scientific theories they appropriated, including physiology, bacteriology, embryology, heredity, and eugenics. Contrary to previous scholarship that does not frame free-love as a movement, *Evolutionary Rhetoric* argues that recognizing free-love feminists' work as comprising a social movement is made uniquely possible by "reading their acts from a rhetorical perspective," asserting that although free-love feminists may have lacked a focused political, economic, or legal agenda, they nevertheless produced a body of rhetoric made cohesive through strategic uptakes of emerging scientific discourse (17). Rhetorical theorists are mentioned sparingly (Bitzer and Burke are paraded momentarily early on), but it is Stephen Toulmin's argument model that molds the majority of Hayden's analysis. Therefore a central contribution of the research is a fascinating *rhetorical* analysis and historical recovery of women's 19th century feminist activity.

Hayden's introduction builds a sturdy case for the merit of her research amongst extant free-love scholarship and swiftly overviews the book's organization. Describing the biographies of free-love feminist leaders in the first chapter, Hayden shows how the domestic experiences of free-love feminists often shaped their sociopolitical stances and rhetorical strategies. For example, having survived an abusive husband, several miscarriages, poverty, and eventually physical disabilities, Rachel Campbell focused her work on attacking social, legal, and economic systems that precluded women's equal treatment. Inspired by secretly reading anatomy textbooks, Mary Gove Nichols pursued education in physical health and utilized a historically powerful metaphor from her involvement in reform physiology to problematize marriage as a "diseased" institution. Similarly, other free-love feminists introduced new terminology such as *heism* and *manism*, while also working to denaturalize understandings of morality and purity. Thus Hayden clearly explains how and why free-love feminists sought to reform oppressive systems of marriage, labor, and women's healthcare by connecting biographical information, issue selection, and rhetorical strategies. In addition to enlarging our history of female rhetors, such work contributes to scholarship seeking to reclaim feminist uses of domestic experiences and patriarchal language.

The second chapter (re)traces free-love feminists' utilization and appropriation of emerging scientific theory. A quote from a 1900 advertisement for *Lucifer the Light Bearer* underscores and foreshadows the disastrous implications of the free-love feminist assertion that "the greatest right of all rights [is] to be born well" (1). Free-love feminists took fresh conclusions from Darwin's theory of sexual selection and redressed marriage as an unnatural institution preventing the necessary, natural process of female choice in mate-selection. By scaffolding their arguments within the hierarchical organization of natural processes, free-love feminists were able to frame their position as promoting better reproduction for society according to new science. Such strategy enabled them to extend their logic to arguments on birth control, marital rape, and abortion. Further, identifying sexual selection as integral to effective reproduction allowed free-love feminists to reposition women's agency as essential, rather than destructive, to social advancement.

As the study of physiology developed in the nineteenth-century, women encountered a bounty of information about their bodies, personal hygiene, diet, and—most popularly—sex and reproduction. Chapter three recovers debates in physiology on whether or not bodies functioned as systems of parts (a mechanist view) or as an expression of a "life force" (a vitalist view). These debates led to a popular view emphasizing "the mind's power in producing sexual feelings in the body" (82). Hayden shows how free-love feminists seized the opportunity to influence debates on psychological health and prioritize the female psyche in health discussions. Emphasizing the relationship between the mind and body also helped feminists position "sexuality as a natural sign of health" and, in turn, recognize sexual pleasure as ordinary if not requisite in sexual reproduction (83). By highlighting the ways in which marital rape damaged physiological health, free-love leaders were able to infuse medical conversations regarding women's bodies with rights discourse.

Chapter four describes how advances in bacteriology influenced various perspectives on women's bodies and sexual health. Discoveries about microbes and germs refuted ideas that women inherently carried venereal disease, calling the seemingly natural and inconsequential promiscuity of men into question. Enriched understandings of disease transmission relocated human agency in health responsibility and helped free-love feminists articulate a need for better health and sex education. Some rhetors drew upon the language of bacteriology to mobilize a metaphor damning the institution of marriage itself as diseased.

Chapters five and six tell the intriguing story of how innovations in embryology and heredity sciences informed free-love feminist rhetoric. Scientists believed the chronological phases of embryologic development represented corresponding phases of human evolution, placing the potential for humanity to progress square in the wombs of women, "literally the setting where evolution would take place" (145). Thus embryonic development became an expression of humanity's health. Embryology's growing popularity provided a scientific warrant for those asserting woman's right to a happy pregnancy and life. Advancements in the science of heredity, namely on acquired characteristics, supplemented increasingly evolutionary-focused scientific discourse. Creating stronger children meant cultivating strong adults, and in arguments on heredity free-love feminists found urgency. The importance of raising intelligent, capable offspring grew in popularity, making space for eugenic ideas that some people ought to reproduce and not others. Hayden rightly cites the "eugenic shift" in free-love feminist rhetoric for halting the movement's momentum and credibility. Free-love feminists began to champion applications of science that progressed the human race during a time when that meant cultivating better white, educated citizens. In turning to eugenics claims, free-love feminists excluded women of color and marginalized impoverished groups who might have otherwise participated and contributed to the movement. As free-love discourse turned increasingly eugenic, its rhetors dismissed racist implications and prioritized white female agency.

The limitations of the book are minimal. Hayden states clearly that the free-love movement was "exclusively white" and rightly differentiates between the institutionally constructed sexualities of white and black women, noting that "slavery had promoted black women's sexual availability rather than restricted their sexuality to certain frameworks" (3). However, it is not clearly shown *how* or *why* those specific sexual frameworks prevented movement leaders from including black women in their work. There is sufficient existing feminist rhetorical scholarship on that historical exclusion for her to have done so. Moreover, on the bottomless issue of nineteenth-century racism, Hayden dips only a toe. If deepening the text's analysis of white feminist racism fell outside the scope of Hayden's project, then an important opportunity to enrich our understanding of the impactful relationship between eugenic discourse and enduring racist ideology remains unfortunately unexamined. Hayden's work is a wonderful effort in feminist scholarship, but falls just short of contemporary intersectional expectations for it to more critically broach the subject of race.

Evolutionary Rhetoric should be known to readers interested in nineteenth-century science, activism, social uptakes of evolutionary theories, feminist rhetoric, and/or women's history more generally, because it contributes important insights to an ongoing effort to recover women's activist histories in feminist and rhetorical arenas. Moreover, Hayden's arguments suggest the power of scientific rationality in sociopolitical activism and further displace the notion that feminists cannot or should not appropriate that power. Hayden skillfully restores the significance of free-love feminist activity, illuminating the historical rhetorical prowess of nineteenth-century women. In her rendering one finds an accessible, well-written demonstration of the value in recovering women's rhetoric.

Minneapolis, Minnesota

Understanding the Essay, edited by Patricia Foster and Jeff Porter. Peterborough, ON: Broadview P, 2012. 261 pp.

Reviewed by Madeline Walker, University of Victoria

Understanding the Essay is an anthology of nineteen critical pieces on how to read and understand the essay, bookended by co-editor Jeff Porter's introduction and a useful compendium of terms relevant to the essay. This book is a valuable contribution to essay studies and a spirited effort to give the essay a more stable literary status and pull it into the academic center from the margins. Each author offers commentary on how to read a chosen essay (which is not included in the volume), and each commentary is an essay in its own right. However, the best critical essays in the book—and I will use this term to differentiate from the source essays—are those by writers who do not veer too sharply into the characteristic digressions of the personal essay but balance their own reading experience with critical analysis.

The editors choose not to qualify the word *essay* in their title with *personal*, as Phillip Lopate did in his 1994 anthology, *The Art of the Personal Essay*. They seem to do this for the sake of capaciousness and simplicity. The term *essay* is notoriously loose, covering everything from the five paragraph academic essay we assign in middle school English, to the journalistic essay found in the pages of the *New Yorker*, to the personal and literary essays of E.B. White and George Orwell. Thus, by using "essay" unadorned, Foster and Porter can include responses to a range of writing: contributors examine, for example, the half-page minimalist "On Trout" by Anne Carson; the sprawling 100-page "A Supposedly Fun Thing I'll Never Do Again" by David Foster Wallace; the transparently political and anti-imperialist Mark Twain piece, "To the Person Sitting in Darkness," about colonization in the Philippines; and the highly personal "Under the Influence" by Scott Russell Sanders about his alcoholic father. Similarly, the critical essays are written in a wide range of styles and forms, from the highly structured analysis of Orwell's "A Hanging" by Carl H. Klaus, to the relaxed synaptic form of Marilyn Abildskov's reading of Woolf's "Street Haunting," and to Sara Levine's polemical, mirroring response to Joy Williams's diatribe, "The Case Against Babies." The simple and engaging cover of this little volume—three origami animals against a yolk-yellow background—disguises its scope and complexity.

Between these covers lie some hits and some misses. Jeff Porter's readable introduction is the first hit. Co-editor Patricia Foster prefaces each critical essay with a short biography of the essayist under consideration; some bios hit the mark while others miss as she tries to capture the essence of each essayist. The critical essays themselves are mostly compelling. The useful "key terms" section closing the book is another hit, with twenty-two clear definitions of terminology important to the essay, such as *double vantage point* and *persona*.

In his introduction, Porter provides a delightful history and poetics of the essay, focusing on the "father of the essay," Michel de Montaigne, and his English counterparts (Bacon, Lamb, and Hazlitt). His main goal in this introduction, however, is to capture the "whatness" of the essay. In this genre that has spanned centuries, what is it that links Montaigne's essays to contemporary pieces by, say, David Foster Wallace? To get at the essay's essence, Porter then describes three salient characteristics of the form: first, the showcasing of the writerly "I" voice, a created persona that establishes intimacy with an imagined reader and is at times unruly, combative, friendly, ironic, or humorous; second, the essay's imitation of the digressive mind—creating the effect of the "mind on the page" (xxiv); and finally, the subversiveness of the genre both in form (i.e., twisting and turning) and content (e.g., the perverse and uncanny are frequent features in essays). As such, argues Porter, the essay as individual mindscape offers a refuge to readers across the centuries as we enjoy wandering with essayists through unpredictable and often unusual terrain—a landscape providing flashes of insight around corners, recognition or re-knowings, and "vertical drops" (moments of self-disclosure, as described in "key terms") along the way. The introduction paves the way for readers to understand the emphases of the contributions that follow, as many of them refer to those three elements.

Most of the critical essays are very strong, but my favorites are those where contributors, seasoned reader-writers, describe revelations about misreading their chosen essays. In other words, we get to experience the "vertical drop" of the critical essayist's move to self-disclosure about his or her own failures as a reader. Porter points out in the introduction that the anthology is about the relationship between close reading and writing, and this is illustrated in many of the critical essays. Foster questions if she's been misreading Didion's essay as she revisits "Georgia O'Keeffe" after twenty years with a more critical eye and a matured sense of class-consciousness. Once considering Didion a feminist heroine, Foster now sees elitism behind Didion's oversimplified portrait of the painter, an elitism that erases O'Keeffe's life from her art. Similarly, after thirty years of teaching "A Hanging," Carl H. Klaus describes his growing uneasiness about his simplification of this canonical Orwell essay. His growing awareness of a split point of view in the essay leads him to a reassessment of both the essay and Orwell. His closing, a warning that we should not reduce essays to a thesis nor assume the truthfulness of the narrator, is worth the price of the book, in my opinion. As a final example of misreading, Lopate admits in his critical essay that after teaching Hazlitt's "On the Pleasure of Hating" twenty times, he realized he had missed something central to the essay: it's not really about hating, it's about "our inability to sustain enthusiasm" (200). Lopate "harps" on this recognition because it took so long for him to recognize that Hazlitt had veered away from his original premise, and the implicit message is that it pays to read and re-read an essay especially closely. It's a tricky genre.

The few misses in the volume are due, I think, to writers veering too sharply into the territory of personal essay in their critiques. Although I acknowledge that these responses are essays in their own right, I believe that we as readers still bring certain expectations to critical analyses, such as a balance of critique with personal experience, some principle of organization, and some kind of thesis. Despite a promising introduction, Robin Hemley, for example, does not manage to lift Twain's essay about the Philippines into relevance for most readers; moreover, he doesn't really get to the point. Similarly, Marilyn Abildskov, in her critical essay on Woolf, is as digressive as Woolf herself. Although some wandering is permitted in a critical analysis, I think readers appreciate a deliberate course. These misses, though, are infrequent and do not detract from the overall value of the volume.

My final caveat about this volume is the absence of the essays under observation. Luckily, Lopate's own volume, *The Art of the Personal Essay*, contains six of them and several others are in the public domain; however, I hunted down the rest through the library and time-consuming interlibrary loans. I wondered about Porter's comment that "this collection is designed to serve as a companion to your favorite anthology of essayists" (xxiii) when no such complete anthology exists, to my knowledge. The absence of the essays under review may create a problem for teachers assigning the book in the writing classroom. Although including all of the original essays may not have been economically or materially feasible, perhaps producing a volume with fewer critical essays along with the appraised essays would be more commercially viable.

Quibbles aside, I find this book compelling because the editors and authors continually show new facets of this enduring form. Even the most seasoned reader-teacher-writers contributing to the book discover and share with us something they hadn't noticed during previous readings; these discoveries deepen, for me, the mystery and beauty of the essay. It also reminds those who teach the essay—both how to read it and how to write it—that its provisional nature is like the facets of a gem. Just keep turning it around in the light.

Victoria, British Columbia

Work Cited

Lopate, Phillip, ed. *The Art of the Personal Essay*. New York: Anchor, 1994. Print.

The WPA Outcomes Statement: A Decade Later, edited by Nicholas N. Behm, Gregory R. Glau, Deborah H. Holdstein, Duane Roen, and Edward M. White. Anderson, SC: Parlor P, 2013. 327 pp.

Reviewed by Courtney Adams Wooten, University of North Carolina at Greensboro

What should first-year writing look like around the United States based on current writing studies research? Edward M. White's similar question on the Writing Program Administrators listserv (WPA-L) in 1996 led to a collaborative effort by some 240 faculty to answer this question. In 2000, the Council of Writing Program Administrators adopted the resulting document, the WPA Outcomes Statement (OS), which set forth common outcomes for first-year writing courses across the U.S. Since then, administrators, WPAs, university faculty, writing instructors, and even students have scrutinized this text. In 2005, *The Outcomes Book: Debate and Consensus after the WPA Outcomes Statement* presented the background and many of the conversations happening about the OS. Susanmarie Harrington states in the introduction to this volume, "The dialogue must continue" (xix), indicating the need for WPAs and writing instructors in particular to continue discussions about national outcomes for first-year writing instruction. *The WPA Outcomes Statement: A Decade Later* does just that, illustrating uses and critiques of the OS more than fifteen years after Edward White's initial question and continuing the conversation about this important document.

The introduction to *The WPA Outcomes Statement* claims that it does not seek to repeat the work done in *The Outcomes Book* of outlining the history and background of the OS. Instead, this volume serves as a "record of how the WPA OS has been adopted, adapted, and modified, and the ways in which the WPA OS is moving outward to affect other parts of the university and university—or college-level—writing instruction" (xii). To this end, *The WPA Outcomes Statement* offers twenty essays organized into three sections, each offering new perspectives on how the OS has been used and in what ways it needs to evolve in order to reflect current research about best practices for first-year college writing. Although there are still many points of difference in first-year writing programs, the OS serves as an important document to codify how composition scholarship can be incorporated into institutional and programmatic decisions about writing instruction. *The WPA Outcomes Statement* presents readers with different ways the OS has been used to support the development and growth of writing programs as well as possible revisions to strengthen the document.

Part one, "Adapting the WPA OS to Develop Curriculum," includes seven perspectives on the OS and curricular development. Debra Frank Dew's "CWPA Outcomes Statement as Heuristic for Inventing Writing-about-Writing Curricula" identifies the OS as a heuristic to support writing-about-writing approaches and help students build transferable writing knowledge. "The Politics of Pedagogy: The Outcomes Statement and Basic Writing" by Wendy Olsen insightfully outlines how the OS reinforces the value of basic writing and articulates connections between basic writing and first-year writing. Kimberly Harrison explains how the OS helped one writing program transition from literature-based first-year writing courses to rhetoric-based courses in "Building a Writing Program with the WPA Outcomes: Authority, Ethos, and Professional Identity." Teresa Grettano, Rebecca Ingalls, and Tracy Ann Morse's valuable contribution, "The Perilous Vision of the Outcomes Statement," complicates Harrison's optimism by emphasizing the limitations of the OS on writing program development, including the possible alienation of faculty who don't identify with rhetoric and composition. "The Outcomes Statement as Support for Teacher Creativity: Applying the WPA OS to Develop Assignments" by Sherry Rankins-Robertson explains how the OS can be used to align writing assignments with outcomes. Broadening the lens, Doug Sweet argues in "Released from the Ghost of Platonic Idealism: How the Outcomes Statement Affirms Rhetorical Curricula" that the OS represents an epistemology of writing that highlights deliberative rhetoric. Finally, Paul Anderson, Chris M. Anson, Martha Townsend, and Kathleen Blake Yancey ask readers to consider what a similar statement for writing across the curriculum programs would look like and why it is needed in "Beyond Composition: Developing a National Outcomes Statement for Writing Across the Curriculum." Taken together, the essays in this section demonstrate some of the advantages and limitations when using the OS to impact curricular developments. Olsen's essay in particular illustrates how the OS can be used to argue for a particular curriculum based on best practices and to create more vertical alignment between writing courses, which positively aligns the writing instruction students receive at different levels.

The eight essays in part two, "Applying the WPA OS to Enact Programmatic, Institutional, and Disciplinary Change," ask readers to consider how the OS can be used for broader change. Craig Jacobsen, Susan Miller-Cochran, and Shelley Rodrigo in "The WPA Outcomes Statement and Disciplinary Authority" explain how the ethos of the OS supported curricular revisions in a ten-campus community college district. Stephen Wilhoit thoughtfully examines how the OS helped to create "deep change" in the way faculty across the curriculum think about writing in "Achieving a Lasting Impact on Faculty Teaching: Using the WPA Outcomes Statement to Develop an Extended

WID Seminar." In "Building Clout in Non-Program Programs by Using the Outcomes Statement," Karen Bishop Morris and Lizbeth A. Bryant explain how the OS reinforced the authority of their "non-program program," or a program that lacks the institutional ethos to impact decisions about the program. Similarly, Darsie Bowden's "Reframing the Conversation: Can the Outcomes Statement Help?" asks WPAs to use the OS to quickly intervene in opportunities to reframe conversations about writing and writing pedagogy. In "The WPA Outcomes Statement: The View from Australia," Susan Thomas relates how the OS helped articulate first-year writing in Australia and strengthened this enterprise. Morgan Gresham's "Ripple Effect: Adopting and Adapting the WPA Outcomes" provides—like Grettano, Ingalls, and Morse—a moment of reflection about potential problems with the OS, describing how it both helped establish an eportfolio assessment and created conflicts with contingent faculty fearful of change. Deirdre Pettipiece and Justin Everett further describe in "Ethos and Topoi: Using the Outcomes Statement Rhetorically To Achieve the Centrality and Autonomy of Writing Programs" how the OS can create both possibilities and dissent in writing programs, which ultimately split their writing program from the English department. Finally, J. S. Dunn et al. recount in "Adoption, Adaptation, Revision: Waves of Collaborative Change at a Large University Writing Program" how the OS has been used and adapted in various ways through different stages of one writing program's development. These essays show how the OS transforms to support different efforts that strengthen writing programs. The OS does not unilaterally create consensus within writing programs about the direction first-year writing should take; instead, it provides a touchstone for changes that locally can look very different.

Finally, the five essays in part three, "Cultivating the Intellectual Enrichment of the WPA OS through Critique," urge readers to see the OS as a living, evolving document. Paul Kei Matsuda and Ryan Skinnell's "Considering the Impact of the WPA Outcomes Statement on Second Language Writers" critiques the monolingual assumptions undergirding the OS, arguing that all students would benefit from a global context. In "Competing Discourses within the WPA Outcomes Statement" Judy Holiday claims that "little rhetoric," or language use in specific situations, needs to be integrated under "big rhetoric," or language use in specific social and historical contexts, in both the OS and writing programs. In "Is Rhetorical Knowledge the Über-Outcome?" Barry M. Maid and Barbara J. D'Angelo explain their adaption of the OS for a technical communication program and the prominence of rhetorical knowledge outcomes in students' reflections, asking if, in fact, this is a role rhetorical knowledge should play. Michael Callaway argues in "The WPA Learning Outcomes: What Role Should Technology Play?" that the technology plank of the OS, added in 2008, inadequately addresses the complex rhetorical situations of writing on screen. Finally, Emily Isaacs and Melinda Knight's "Assessing the Impact of the Outcomes Statement" presents sobering findings; out of 101 institutions they studied, only 15 have programs or courses that align with the OS and, generally, "the WPA OS has not been broadly adopted or even adapted by our nation's colleges and universities" (300). The OS has space to evolve as it attempts to satisfy the diverse interests of many scholars and to provide guidance for first-year writing programs, but the WPA community must ultimately resolve these different directions into a document that remains functional.

Isaacs and Knight's conclusions about the lack of attention to the OS call into question its prominence, particularly as the OS has received attention from many composition scholars. As we participate in conversations about the OS, there are fundamental questions to answer. First, do Isaacs and Knight's conclusions hold up with larger samples of institutions and in institutions we are familiar with? Second, if so, do we need to focus more on promoting the OS to these institutions and programs? The conversations represented in *The WPA Outcomes Statement* valuably demonstrate various ways the OS can be used and adapted. However, a crucial conversation to begin is how writing programs work toward or fight against the idea of universal outcomes. By and large, authors in this collection do not resist the OS as a set of national outcomes that should guide their writing programs. The relatively small number of writing programs that have adopted or adapted the OS indicates that many are either unfamiliar with the OS or resist the standardization that it represents. The creators of this document actively sought to create a set of outcomes that writing programs could adapt to their local conditions, but the OS still offers particular perspectives about first-year writing that are not universally accepted or taught. This book illustrates some of the work that has already been done with the OS and asks us to consider what work is left to do in order for the OS to reach its potential as a representation of national outcomes for first-year writing.

Greensboro, North Carolina

Work Cited

Harrington, Susanmarie, Keith Rhodes, Ruth Overman Fischer, and Rita Malenczyk, eds. *The Outcomes Book: Debate and Consensus after the WPA Outcomes Statement.* Logan, UT: Utah SUP, 2005. Print.

Announcements

CFP for Special Issue of *Composition Studies*
Theme: Comics, Multimodality, and Composition
For 43.1 (Spring 2015)
Guest Editor: Dale Jacobs, University of Windsor

Description

Over the past ten years, composition has increasingly embraced writing and reading in multiple modes (words, but also images, sounds, video, spatial relationships, gestures, and other sign systems). In this movement towards multimodality, comics have been largely ignored. Comics, however, provide rich ground for exploration in relation to multimodality and composition. This special issue begins with the idea that comics are a valuable space of practice for multimodal literacies, both inside and outside the classroom.

Like other multimodal texts, comics form a multifaceted environment in which meaning is negotiated between creators and readers. Comics add another dimension to multimodality, which has often focused on digital texts, and can be used to link traditional alphabetic literacies with newer digital ones. Furthermore, as Michael Bitz argues in *When Commas Meet Kryptonite: Classroom Lessons from the Comic Book Project*, "In the context of new media and literacies, comics are a rare bridge between the canon of reading skills that children are expected to master in school and the literacies that they embrace on their own and out of school" (11). Not only are comics important multimodal texts in their own right, but they can also function as an important bridge to other literacies both inside and outside the classroom.

This special issue of *Composition Studies* will explore how comics can be productively used in writing theory and practice. Articles, sequential narratives, short reflective essays, and Course Designs are all welcome, as are pieces on comics aimed at the "Composing With" section of the journal. Possible topics include (but are not limited to):

- Comics as a way to connect reading and composing multimodal texts.
- Comics literacies and digital literacies.
- Comics in relation to the *NCTE Position Statement on Multimodal Literacies*, the *WPA Outcomes Statement*, and/or the *Framework for Success in Postsecondary Writing*.
- Comics and/as collaboration.
- Comics, rhetoric, and the teaching of writing.
- Comics theory and the teaching of writing.
- Comics as a way to examine how students conceive and experience literacies outside of school and possible connections to school literacies.

- Specific ways to use comics in the composition classroom.
- Examinations of how Comics Studies can inform Composition Studies and vice versa

Timeline

Full-length submissions due **August 1, 2014**
Submission determinations sent by **November 1, 2014**
Revised manuscripts due **February 13, 2015**

Contacts

Direct queries about the special issue and full-length manuscripts in .doc or .docx formats to Dale Jacobs at djacobs@uwindsor.ca.
- Direct general questions about *Composition Studies* to compstudies@uc.edu. Visit our website for more information: http://www.uc.edu/journals/composition-studies.html.

Community Literacy Journal: Call for Submissions

The peer-reviewed *Community Literacy Journal* seeks contributions for upcoming issues. At *CLJ*, we understand "community literacy" as the domain for literacy work that exists outside of mainstream educational and work institutions. It can be found in programs devoted to adult education, early childhood education, reading initiatives, lifelong learning, workplace literacy, or work with marginalized populations, but it can also be found in more informal, *ad hoc* projects. We welcome submission that address any social cultural, rhetorical, or institutional aspects of community literacy; we particularly welcome co-authored pieces in collaboration with community partners.

Possible articles and approaches include, but are not limited to:
- What are the broad, disciplinary implications and possibilities for emerging community-literacy initiatives at the programmatic and institutional levels?
- How are the rhetorical features of oral, written, and visual curricula negotiated and transformed in academic-community collaborations?
- To what extent will it become important–or not–to distinguish between "community literacy" and "service learning"?
- What roles will writing-program administrators play in supporting community-literacy efforts?
- What is the place of community literacy in "managed" and market-principle driven universities?

For more information about *Community Literacy Journal* and submission guidelines, please visit our website at http://www.communityliteracy.org.

Contributors

Amanda Athon is a PhD candidate in her final year of the Rhetoric and Writing Program at Bowling Green State University. Her most recent project explores how students with diverse language backgrounds experience the assessment process.

William Duffy is an assistant professor of English at the University of Memphis. His course design essay was composed while on the faculty at Francis Marion University.

Oriana Gatta is a rhetoric and composition PhD candidate in Georgia State University's English Department. Her research interests include visual rhetoric/culture, feminist theory/pedagogy, critical theory/pedagogy, digital media/pedagogy, and comics studies. Her dissertation addresses the visual rhetorical construction of ideology in comics.

Michelle Gibson is Professor Emerita of the Department of Women's, Gender, and Sexuality Studies at the University of Cincinnati. Her scholarship focuses on sexuality studies and pedagogy. She is co-author (with Jonathan Alexander and Deborah Meem) of *Finding Out: An Introduction to LGBT Studies*, now in its second edition. In retirement, she writes the blog ProfSpazz at http://profspazz.com.

Danielle Hartke is a graduate student in rhetoric and composition at the University of Wisconsin–Milwaukee. Her research interests include composition pedagogy, visuality and rhetoric, artist statements, feminist theory, second language writing, and rhetoric of science. In her spare time, she can be found rock climbing.

Michael Madson is a doctoral student at the University of Minnesota–Twin Cities. He teaches second language writing courses and studies the intersections of culture, technology, and literacy.

Dan Martin is a full time faculty member in the Writing and Rhetoric Department at the University of Central Florida where he has taught mostly composition courses for the past ten years. His research interests include WAC, composition theory, intertexuality, and writing and technology.

Patricia Mellon Moore, an adjunct instructor at Peublo Community College, will receive her MA in English from Colorado State University—Pueblo in spring 2014. Prior publications include poetry, fiction, and creative non-fiction.

Sushil K. Oswal researches in the areas of digital media, technology, and accessibility. Oswal's work has appeared in *Kairos*, *Journal of Business and Technical Communication*, *Technical Communication Quarterly*, *ATTW Bulletin*, *Business Communication Quarterly*, *Profession*, and several edited collections.

Brian Ray is Assistant Professor of English at the University of Nebraska at Kearney. His work has appeared in the *Journal of Basic Writing*, *Composition Studies*, *Computers and Composition*, and *Rhetoric Review*.

Martha Wilson Schaffer is a third year student in the Bowling Green State University rhetoric and writing program and a mentor to new graduate teaching assistants in the General Studies Writing Program. Her research interests include affect theory and ethics of care in writing studies, legal writing, and the role of rhetoric in social justice.

Jacqueline Schiappa is a graduate instructor and doctoral candidate in the Department of Writing Studies at the University of Minnesota. Her work is grounded in feminist and rhetorical theory, and her dissertation explores relationship(s) between social movements and social media activism.

Madeline Walker teaches writing to nurses at the University of Victoria. She holds a PhD in American literature. Her first academic book, *The Trouble with Sauling Around*, was published by University of Iowa Press in 2011. Her first book of poetry will be published by Demeter Press in 2014.

Courtney Adams Wooten is a doctoral candidate in English with a specialization in rhetoric and composition at the University of North Carolina at Greensboro. Her research focuses on literacy learning that occurs in liminal educational spaces outside of institutions but under their purview.

Adopt the *MLA Handbook* for Your Fall or Spring Classes.

Check It Out.

MLA members can request a complimentary copy at **www.mla.org**. Each copy includes print and online formats.

Assign It.

Your students can start using the *Handbook* the day you assign it. They can buy access online at **www.mlahandbook.org** (a print copy will be mailed to them) or purchase a print copy online or at their local bookstore (each print copy comes with an online-access code).

Recipient of *Choice* Award for Outstanding Academic Title

The searchable Web site features

- the full text of the *MLA Handbook*
- over two hundred additional examples
- research project narratives, with sample papers

xxii & 292 pp.
Paper 978-1-60329-024-1 $22.00

A large-print edition is also available.

www.mlahandbook.org

Phone orders 646 576-5161 ■ Fax 646 576-5160 ■ www.mla.org

How does the MLA work for you?

Promotes the study of language and literature

Publishes your scholarship

Hosts an annual convention where you can share your work

Compiles the *Job Information List*

Creates opportunities for scholarly interaction—visit the new *MLA Commons*

The Modern Language Association is a community of nearly 28,000 members dedicated to strengthening the study and teaching of language and literature. The MLA makes it possible for you to

- search the MLA *Job Information List* at no charge
- read reports and surveys issued by the MLA on the job market, enrollments, evaluating scholarship, and the state of scholarly publishing
- benefit from public outreach activities, including the popular MLA Language Map
- download the Academic Workforce Advocacy Kit, a tool for helping improve conditions for teachers and students
- access the *MLA Handbook* Web site and FAQs about MLA style

Become an MLA member at www.mla.org and receive the following benefits:

- subscriptions to *PMLA* and the *MLA Newsletter*
- access to directories of members and departmental administrators
- a 20% discount on all MLA titles
- ability to read the *ADE Bulletin* or *ADFL Bulletin* online and search bulletin archives if your department is a member of the ADE or ADFL
- the *MLA Directory of Periodicals*, a searchable database that provides subscription information for over 4,000 journals in the humanities

Three easy ways to join:

▲ Visit **www.mla.org**.
▲ E-mail **membership@mla.org** to request a membership packet.
▲ Call 646 576-5151.

**The MLA Annual Convention
9–12 January 2014
in Chicago**

featuring the presidential theme
Vulnerable Times

Join us at the largest gathering of teachers and scholars in the humanities for

- roundtables, workshops, and discussion
- special presentations featuring renowned thinkers, artists, and critics in conversation
- local excursions for registrants

2014 members receive reduced rates and special discounts for the 2014 convention in Chicago.

Visit **www.mla.org/convention** for more information.

www.mla.org

#mlanews
#mlaconvention

Just published in the MLA series
Approaches to Teaching
WORLD LITERATURE

Approaches to Teaching the Works of Italo Calvino

Edited by **Franco Ricci**

"The volume's readability and bibliographic and pedagogical detail and each essay's careful framework render the volume valuable for nonspecialists, for Italianists, and for Calvino specialists, too."

—*Tommasina Gabriele*
Wheaton College, Massachusetts

NEW Now available
vi & 159 pp. • 6 x 9 • Cloth $37.50 • Paper $19.75

Approaches to Teaching the Works of Carmen Martín Gaite

Edited by **Joan L. Brown**

"This is an excellent and welcome book, written with care by a diverse group of scholars. Readers will find many innovative teaching techniques and activities to enhance the learning experience for students; the reviews of Martín Gaite's works and of the critical studies on her will broaden the professor's understanding."

—*Catherine G. Bellver*
University Nevada, Las Vegas

NEW

Now available
xii & 280 pp. • 6 x 9 • Cloth $37.50 • Paper $19.75

Modern Language Association **MLA**

Phone orders 646 576-5161 ■ Fax 646 576-5160 ■ www.mla.org

Rhetoric & Writing PhD Program

Preparing Rhetoric and Composition Faculty for over 30 Years

Since its founding in 1980, Bowling Green State University's program has prepared about ninety graduates for faculty careers in rhetoric and composition. Students and faculty in the Rhetoric & Writing PhD Program are committed scholar-teachers who utilize a range of approaches—rhetorical, cultural, empirical, technological—that characterize rhetoric and composition in the twenty-first century.

Some highlights of the Rhetoric & Writing PhD Program:
- Eight core courses in history, theory, digital rhetorics, research methods, scholarly publication, and composition studies as a discipline, plus electives in rhetoric and composition and related areas of scholarly interest to students.
- Professional development involving mentoring, collaboration, a monthly colloquium series, and post-prelim groups emphasizing dissertation progress and the job search.
- Varied assistantship assignments (FYW, intermediate writing, writing center, faculty research, editorial work, program administration, community outreach, etc.) and competitive non-service fellowships in the fourth year of funding.
- Four-year graduation rate typical for full-time students.
- Placement rate among program graduates approaching 100%.

Rhetoric & Writing PhD Program
http://www.bgsu.edu/departments/english/rcweb/index.html
Facebook Group: BGSU Rhetoric & Writing

Program Director, Sue Carter Wood
carters@bgsu.edu
English Graduate Office: 419-372-6864

STUDY
COMPOSITION
AND RHETORIC

UNIVERSITY OF MICHIGAN

SCHOOL OF EDUCATION

DEPARTMENT of ENGLISH

Joint PhD Program in English and Education

Bringing together the best of research, scholarship, and pedagogy from both English and Education, this interdisciplinary program draws on top-flight resources to provide a satisfying and rich doctoral experience. Among our strengths, we offer a supportive and engaging community of scholars that includes both students and faculty, and we provide the flexibility for students to craft a program centered on their individual interests. These interests have included rhetorical theory, literacy studies, new media composition, applied linguistics, English language studies, teacher education, and writing assessment; our faculty are happy to work with you to craft a program centered on your research and teaching interests.

This PHD program is designed for students who hold master's degrees in English or education and who have teaching experience. We have an excellent record of placing graduates in tenure-track positions in education and English departments in colleges and universities.

Phone: 734.763.6643 • Email: ed.jpee@umich.edu

soe.umich.edu/jpee

Education Faculty

Chandra L. Alston: teacher education, English education, adolescent literacy, urban education

Barry Fishman: technology, video games as models for learning, reform involving technology, teacher learning, design-based implementation research

Elizabeth Birr Moje: adolescent and disciplinary literacy, literacy and cultural theory, research methods

Mary J. Schleppegrell: functional linguistics, second language learning, discourse analysis, language development

Co-Chairs

Anne Curzan: history of English, language and gender, corpus linguistics, lexicography, pedagogy

Anne Ruggles Gere: composition theory, gender and literacy, writing assessment, and pedagogy

English Faculty

David Gold: history of rhetoric, women's rhetorics, composition pedagogy

Scott Richard Lyons: Native American and global indigenous studies, settler colonialism, posthumanism

Alisse Portnoy: rhetoric and composition, rhetorical activism and civil rights movements

Megan Sweeney: African American literature and culture, ethnography, pedagogy, critical prison studies

Melanie R. Yergeau: composition and rhetoric, digital media studies, disability studies, autistic culture

PARLOR PRESS
EQUIPMENT FOR LIVING

New Releases Fall 2013

A Rhetoric for Writing Program Administrators
Edited by Rita Malenczyk. 471 pages.
Thirty-two contributors delineate the major issues and questions in the field of writing program administration and provide readers new to the field with theoretical lenses through which to view major issues and questions.

Writing Program Administration and the Community College
Heather Ostman. 241 pages.
From the history of the community college in the United States to current issues and concerns facing writing programs and their administrators and instructors, *Writing Program Administration and the Community College* offers a comprehensive look into writing programs at the public two-year institutions.

Recently Released . . .

The WPA Outcomes Statement—A Decade Later
Edited by Nicholas N. Behm, Gregory R. Glau, Deborah H. Holdstein, Duane Roen, and Edward M. White.

Writing Program Administration at Small Liberal Arts Colleges
Jill M. Gladstein and Dara Rossman Regaignon.

Rewriting Success in Rhetoric and Composition Careers
Edited by Amy Goodburn, Donna LeCourt, and Carrie Leverenz.

and with the WAC Clearinghouse . . .

Writing Programs Worldwide: Profiles of Academic Writing in Many Places
Edited by Chris Thaiss, Gerd Bräuer, Paula Carlino, Lisa Ganobcsik-Williams, and Aparna Sinha

International Advances in Writing Research: Cultures, Places, Measures
Edited by Charles Bazerman, Chris Dean, Jessica Early, Karen Lunsford, Suzie Null, Paul Rogers, and Amanda Stansell

www.parlorpress.com

www.ingramcontent.com/pod-product-compliance
Lightning Source LLC
Chambersburg PA
CBHW031323160426
43196CB00007B/644